The English Church

The English Church

*Tim Tatton-Brown
and John Crook*

NEW HOLLAND

First published in 2005 by New Holland Publishers (UK) Ltd
London • Cape Town • Sydney • Auckland

10 9 8 7 6 5 4 3 2 1

www.newhollandpublishers.com

Garfield House, 86–88 Edgware Road, London W2 2EA, United Kingdom

80 McKenzie Street, Cape Town 8001, South Africa

14 Aquatic Drive, Frenchs Forest, NSW 2086, Australia

218 Lake Road, Northcote, Auckland, New Zealand

ISBN 1 84330 965 3

Publishing Manager: Jo Hemmings
Senior Editor: Kate Michell
Editor: Sarah Larter
Assistant Editor: Kate Parker
Designer & Cover Design: Alan Marshall
Production: Joan Woodroffe
Cartography: William Smuts
Index: Dorothy Frame

Reproduction by Pica Digital (Pte) Ltd, Singapore
Printed and bound in Singapore by Kyodo Printing Co.
(Singapore) Pte Ltd

COVER AND PRELIMINARY PAGES

FRONT COVER: St George's, Dunster.

SPINE: All Saints', Hillesden.

BACK COVER: *top left*: St Andrew's, Cullompton; *top right*: St Mary's, Warwick;
bottom left: St Helen's, Brant Broughton; *bottom right*: St Mary's, Kempley.

FRONT FLAP: St Mary's, Whitby

BACK FLAP: St Edmund, King and Martyr, Southwold

HALF-TITLE PAGE: One of Maximilien Lott's allegorical figures on Robert
Cecil's tomb in St Etheldreda's, Hatfield.

TITLE SPREAD: St Oswald's, Ashbourne.

RIGHT: The reredos above the high altar at St Peter and St Paul's, Wisbech is a
copy of *The Last Supper* by Salviati of Venice.

PAGE 6: *top*: The tower of St John the Baptist's church, Burford; *bottom left*:
Carving of St Peter on a hammerbeam at St John the Baptist's, Bere Regis;
bottom right: A mosaic from the baptistry of 1896 in St Saviour's, Eastbourne
depicting Oswald planting the Cross at Heavenfield.

PAGE 7: *left*: The spire with external Sanctus bell at St Mary's, Ickleton;
right: Stained glass at St Mary's, Nantwich.

AUTHOR'S ACKNOWLEDGEMENTS

I would like to thank my wife, Veronica, for the word-processing of the
manuscript, assisted by all my children; Kate Michell and all at New Holland
Publishers for providing me with much help and editorial advice, as did John
Crook, the excellent photographer.

AUTHOR'S DEDICATION

For Hugh and Robert.

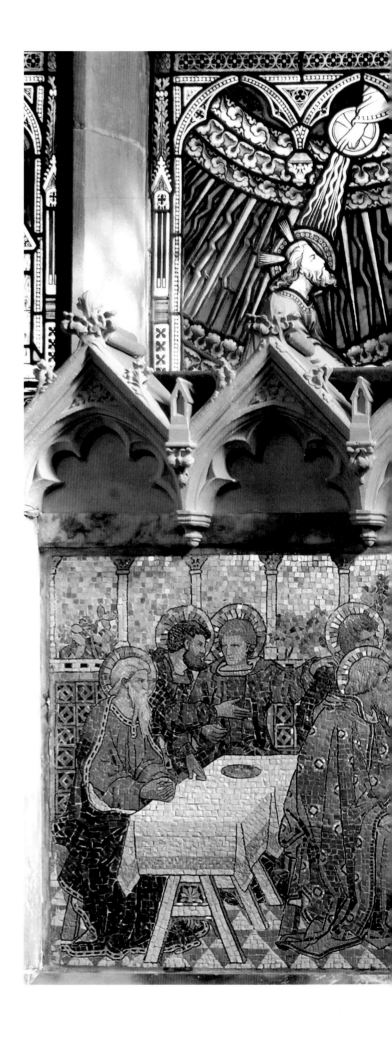

CONTENTS

INTRODUCTION

There are over 18,000 Anglican churches, and almost every village and urban neighbourhood in England still has a church at its core. There are also many other redundant and ruined churches, and even more have been demolished and remain only as archaeological sites. All of these buildings have been the focus of English communities for well over a thousand years, and until the late 20th century were used regularly by almost all the members of the community literally from the cradle to the grave. This may no longer be the case, but the parish church, and all things relating to it, is still the most important source for English local history. Churches are now visited by more strangers from outside the parish than ever before, and even if they do not come as Christians for the services, they come as students and tourists to find out about the history – particularly the medieval history – of the community. Before the Reformation, many churches had vast sums spent on them by the wealthy of the parish, and so churches are the largest source of medieval art and architecture in England.

Most of the earliest churches (apart from a few possible Roman structures) were built in England after the arrival of St Augustine in AD 597, although St Martin's in Canterbury was first built before this. Remarkably, fragments of 7th-century churches still exist, for example at Escomb, Jarrow and Bradwell, although most of these buildings were destroyed by the Vikings. In the late Anglo-Saxon period many new churches were founded and parts of them survive within quite a large number of churches, as at those in Repton, Wing, Deerhurst and Breamore. After the Norman Conquest in 1066, the lords of virtually every manor built a church near their manor house. By the early 12th century these 'manorial chapels' had evolved into the parish churches. The manorial boundaries were also, in most cases, fossilized as the parish boundaries at this time.

During the 12th and 13th centuries, the population of England increased dramatically, and this can be most clearly seen today in the majority of the parish churches where naves were enlarged and aisles were added on either side. At the same time, masons' and carpenters' skills were developing rapidly, and the sturdy but rather crude Romanesque (often called Norman in England) architecture of the 11th and 12th centuries evolved at the end of the 12th century into the Gothic style. Between this time and the early 14th century, architecture developed so rapidly that it is possible to date the masonry very accurately from its style. In the 13th century,

OPPOSITE, BELOW: *The superb 'Breedon Angel' is one of the finest Anglo-Saxon sculptures in the country.*

BELOW LEFT: *The west end of the large, mid-12th-century aisled nave of St Peter's, Northampton.*

BELOW RIGHT: *Medieval stained glass in St Mary's, Fairford; in the bottom left-hand corner a devil can be seen carting off a lost soul in a wheelbarrow.*

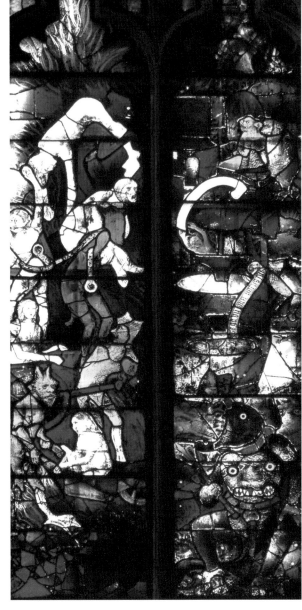

with remarkable features and superb glass and tracery in the windows. This was also when many of the tallest and most elaborate spires were built and when carved decoration was at its best.

Then, when famine and plague, particularly the Black Death of 1348–9, struck England in the later 14th century, between one-third and one-half of the population died. Despite this, a wonderful new style of architecture developed – the Perpendicular – which was quickly used in parish church construction, and more new building work took place. This period saw the construction of chantry chapels for the rich, and during the 15th century many of the churches in the wealthiest communities had their naves completely rebuilt and elaborate chantries installed – Long Melford and Cirencester are just two examples of many. Several churches also rebuilt their chancels as well, after a 'deal' was struck with the patron of the living, for example at Fairford or Salisbury. This was also a time for the building of large west towers and elaborate porches, and by the early 16th century this process had reached another high point, which was rapidly curtailed in the 1530s and 1540s after Henry VIII's break with Rome.

The biggest change for parish churches came, however, soon after the death of Henry in January 1547. On the evening of 8 February, a solemn dirge was held in every parish church and all the bells were tolled. On the following day a requiem mass was offered everywhere for the dead

the eastern, or priests', part of the church underwent a great change as well, and it was at this time that almost all small Norman sanctuaries were replaced with larger, new chancels, containing not only the principal altar, but also many accessories to it and seats for the priests. The chancel was usually separated from the nave by a screen, but the elaborate rood lofts above these screens, with stairs leading up to them, were not created until the late 15th century.

A high point in ecclesiastical architecture was reached in the early 14th century, when some extraordinary new churches were built, for example at Patrington and Nantwich,

monarch's soul. Within a year, however, all this was done away with, as Edward VI ordered that roods and stone altars be 'plucked down' and chantries were abolished. In their place came communion tables, and the pulpit became the focus of the church. Much of the old decoration was destroyed or covered over, for example the wall paintings, but some of the best of what has survived can be seen in this book, for example the stained glass at Fairford and St Neot; the Doom painting at Salisbury; and the statues on the tower of Isle Abbots.

The story since the Reformation is much more complicated, and most churches had their 17th- and 18th-century

ABOVE: *The interior of St Mary's, Whitby, looking east; the old chancel arch can just be seen behind the pulpit and clock.*

RIGHT: *Stained glass designed by Edward Burne-Jones in Lord Salisbury's church of St Etheldreda, Hatfield.*

OPPOSITE: *The magnificent nave, screen and chancel at St Mary Magdalene's, Newark-on-Trent.*

furnishings removed by later 19th-century restorations. A few rare survivals from this period have, however, been included, for example, the nave of Warwick; the wonderful box-pews and galleries within Whitby parish church; and the family pew in Breedon on the Hill. The story has not yet come to an end, and the new and very fine late 19th-century church at Eastbourne is included, as well as the excellent 20th-century engraved glass at Moreton. This is, therefore, just a selection of 100 of the best and most interesting parish churches in England.

TIM TATTON-BROWN

THE SOUTH-WEST

Most of the churches depicted here are major late medieval ones, which display the wealth (particularly from sheep and trading) of the local people. Some of this wealth was spent on spectacular towers, but it was also much used for now-vanished chantries, and the shells of these chapels or whole 'chantry' churches are still beautiful evocative spaces today. The area also includes some magnificent churches of an earlier period, such as the Anglo-Saxon church at Breamore or Norman Tintagel and Studland, and the 12th-century towers at East Meon and Branscombe. Some of the churches owe their being to individuals, such as Elias of Dereham or Bishops Grandison and William of Edington, while others reflect the piety of the wealthy groups of citizens who paid for fine decoration. Finally we have one 18th-century new church, the Framptons' Moreton, which is now filled with magnificent 20th-century engraved clear glass.

RIGHT: *This wonderful hexagonal vault, which has incredibly intricately carved bosses, sits over the north porch of St Mary Redcliffe, Bristol (see pages 60–61).*

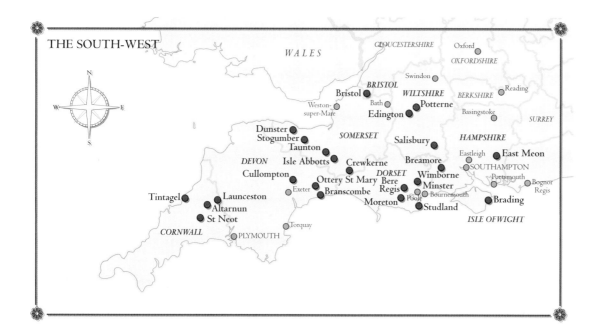

THE SOUTH-WEST

12

ST MATERIANA, TINTAGEL

CORNWALL

Since the 12th century, Tintagel has been famous as the site of King Arthur's mythical castle. Because of these Arthurian associations, Richard, Earl of Cornwall chose to build his own castle on this rugged site on the north Cornish coast in the mid-13th century. Long before this, however, a Dark Age settlement with links to Mediterranean civilization existed here, the remains of which have been uncovered by archaeologists. Recent work suggests that there was a major settlement from the 4th to the 6th centuries AD, which was protected by a strong, ditched fortification. On the flat hilltop, a third of a mile (0.5km) to the south, and very prominently sited, is Tintagel's parish church. It is set within a large graveyard, and archaeological work

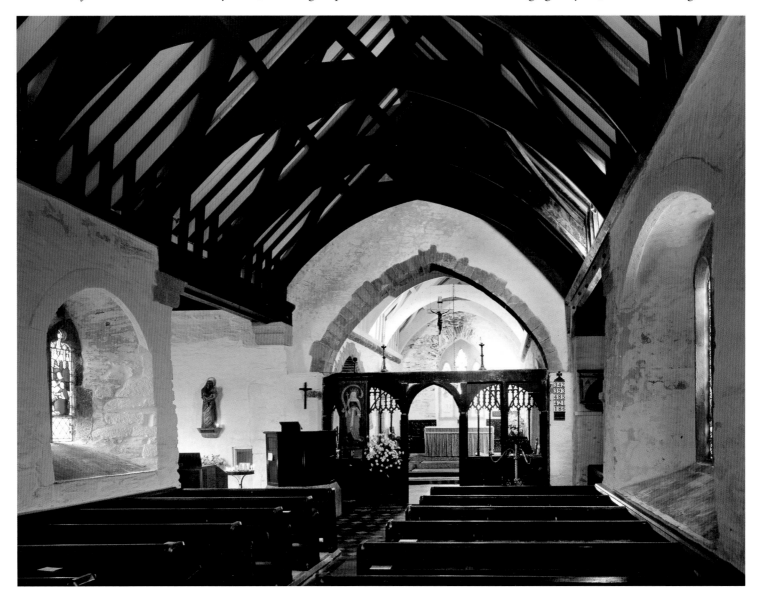

has again shown that some of the low mounds in the churchyard cover a series of graves that may date back as far as the 6th century. Only later, perhaps, was a church built here, although there may have been a monastic cell in the area.

The first church was probably built in the 11th century, when Robert of Mortain, the half-brother of William the Conqueror (1027–87), became the first Norman earl of Cornwall and owned the surrounding manor of Bossiney.

The present parish church is a large cruciform structure that was erected in the 12th century, and was no doubt built for the population of Tintagel and its surrounding hamlets. Many rough features, such as the windows and door-ways, chancel arch and font (which has some grotesque heads carved on it), suggest a late Norman date; but some fragments of the late 11th-century church, for example the nave's north doorway, may still include elements from the earlier church. Sadly, as with many primitive-looking churches, the internal plaster was hacked off the walls during a 19th-century restoration. A large tower was perhaps planned for the crossing in the 12th century, but it seems never to have been finished. Instead, a tower with a crenellated parapet was added to the western end of the church in the 15th century. This is now a major landmark for ships at sea.

The long transepts are an unusual feature of this church and each must have contained two or three altars against their east walls before the Reformation. The transepts were later rebuilt and the south transept was enlarged, and 13th-century lancet windows can be seen in some of the walls. The north window of the north transept was inserted in the early 14th century and the porches on either side of the nave are also of this date. Another interesting feature is the unusual Roman milestone in the south transept.

BELOW: *St Materiana sits atop a wild windswept headland overlooking the Bristol Channel.*

ST ANIETUS, ST NEOT
CORNWALL

BELOW: *The oak branch that projects from the top of St Anietus's tower is renewed each year on Oak Apple Day.*

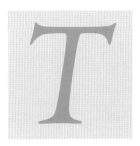

T his magnificent church lies a few miles east of Bodmin in a wooded valley on the southern edge of Bodmin Moor. Inside the church, one of England's finest collections of late medieval and early Tudor stained glass can be seen, despite major restoration and replacement work during the 19th century.

The southern façade of the church, which is seen on approaching the church, is formed from beautifully cut blocks of the local granite, which is known as moorstone. This work continues around the two-storey south porch, and above the whole is a fine crenellated parapet, broken up into bays by pinnacles over smaller crenellations that sit atop the buttresses. The whole of the south aisle dates from the early 15th century, when the 14th-century church was rebuilt. Inside the south porch is a most unusual stone-ribbed tunnel-vault, and beyond it is the very fine original wagon roof of the

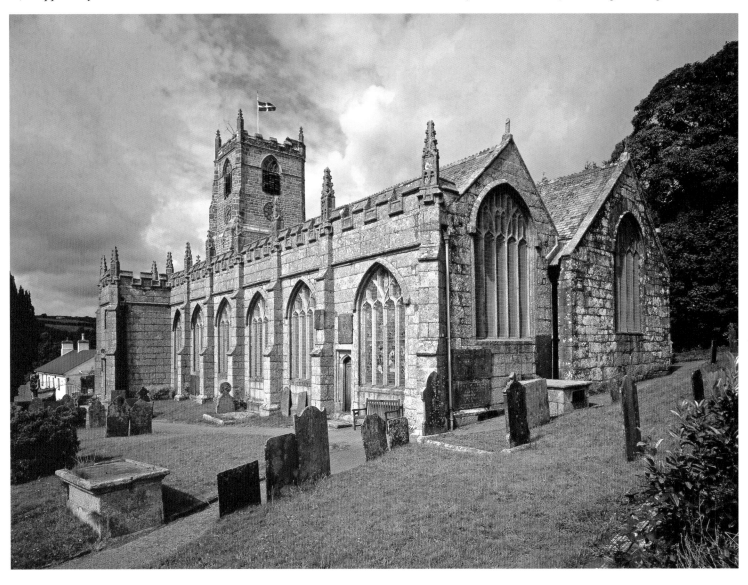

south aisle. In the chancel, something of the 14th-century walls can still be seen, but the north aisle is of a later style, and was probably constructed in about 1520, just before the Reformation.

The great glory of the church is undoubtedly its collection of pre-Reformation windows. However, the glass was subject to some restoration work by John Hedgeland in 1830. The glass has also been moved around, so, for example, the second window east of the porch, which was given by the Calway family, was originally at the eastern end of the north aisle, presumably in their chantry chapel.

The five-light east window of the south aisle – all the other windows are only of four lights – is one of the finest and best preserved. It shows the story of the Creation and is full of remarkable imagery, such as God planning the universe mathematically and Adam and Eve being thrown out of Paradise. The next window on the south shows the story of Noah, with the ark shown as a three-masted ship of the late

medieval period. Most of the other windows in the south aisle depict saints and were donated by local families. In the north aisle, by contrast, is a window given by the young women of the parish, while next to this is a wonderful window depicting the life of St Neot, which was given by the young men of the parish. All these windows merit careful study and it is a miracle that so much ancient glass survived the Reformation.

BELOW LEFT: *The Noah window in the south aisle shows Noah drunk on the ground.*

BELOW: *The church's finest stained-glass window depicts incidents in the life of St Neot.*

ST NONNA, ALTARNUN

CORNWALL

ABOVE AND BELOW:
Detailed carving appears on the bench-ends; this one above shows a fool, while below is a carving with the details of its maker inscribed beneath.

RIGHT: *The nave is lined with strong granite columns leading to a late 15th-century rood screen. Note the surviving Norman font in the foreground.*

This fine church, which has a 109-foot (33-metre) high tower, is situated in a deep valley on the north-eastern side of Bodmin Moor. Below the church is a narrow bridge over Penpont Water, and a picturesque village.

The church is dedicated to the 6th-century Welsh saint who was the mother of St David. She perhaps passed through this village on her way to Brittany from Ireland and Wales. There was clearly an early Christian site here, presumably, as the name of the place suggests, the 'altar set up to St Nonna', and there is still a Celtic cross in the churchyard near the gate. By the 12th century, there must have been a fine Norman church on the site, but this was demolished in the early 15th century, although a few sculptural fragments of the church are found as rubble in the later walls. There is, however, a magnificent Norman font bowl decorated with large bearded heads at each corner with even larger snakes and six-petalled rosettes in between, making the font resemble a large cushion capital.

During the prosperous late Middle Ages, the whole church was rebuilt with a long nave and chancel flanked by north and south arcades with wide arches and large, separately roofed aisles. For all this 15th-century work local moorstone blocks were used, and by this time iron tools of sufficient strength were being made, allowing this very hard granite to be shaped in the characteristic late Perpendicular Cornish style. A form of prefabrication was used to make up the large blocks that were used for bases, monolithic pillars, capitals and arch blocks for the wide, four-centred arches. The granite was also carved for the tracery of the aisle windows. The nave and aisles, and unusually the north and south porches, still have their original 15th-century wagon roofs. At the end of the 15th century, a fine new rood screen was installed, which went right across the nave and the aisles, and allowed access to the rood loft from a stair-turret on the north. This screen was restored in the 1880s, and coved-out timbers for a new rood loft were started at either end, although they were never finished.

In the early 16th century, a new set of benches, which had wonderfully carved ends, was installed. The benches were also completely rebuilt in the late 19th century as new pews. However, seventy-nine of the original bench-ends were kept, and these have many different scenes carved on them, including the instruments of Christ's Passion, which would not have been allowed after the Reformation. One bench-end, which is by the font, reveals the carver's name – Robart Daye.

A magnificent inscribed altar rail, dated 1684, runs across the full width of the church.

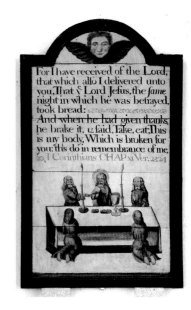

ABOVE: *Dating from 1620, this board in the chancel records and depicts Christ celebrating the Eucharist.*

LEFT: *A truly picturesque parish church, St Nonna's sits above a pretty village and is accessed via a bridge over Penpont Water.*

ST MARY MAGDALENE, LAUNCESTON

CORNWALL

ABOVE: *Carved granite masonry from the early 16th century decorates the north-east corner of the church.*

BELOW: *The oak chancel screen was carved in 1911 by Rashleigh Pinwell; there is also a very fine pre-Reformation pulpit, seen here on the left.*

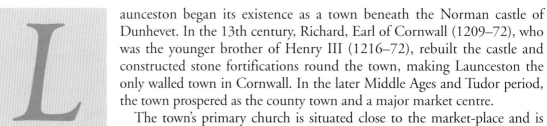

L aunceston began its existence as a town beneath the Norman castle of Dunhevet. In the 13th century, Richard, Earl of Cornwall (1209–72), who was the younger brother of Henry III (1216–72), rebuilt the castle and constructed stone fortifications round the town, making Launceston the only walled town in Cornwall. In the later Middle Ages and Tudor period, the town prospered as the county town and a major market centre.

The town's primary church is situated close to the market-place and is technically a chapel. It was vested in the mayor and burgesses in 1319, and a new church was probably built some time after this. Today, only the detached west tower of this church survives; it was paid for by Edward, the Black Prince (1330–76), who was created the 1st Duke of Cornwall in 1337. The rebuilding seems to have been protracted, and it was completed only in 1380, four years after the death of the Black Prince, when the Bishop of Exeter issued a new 'licence for the performance of Divine worship' to the mayor and burgesses of the town.

Towards the end of the 15th century, a completely new church was contemplated and land was bought to the east of the Norman church in 1467. It was, however, nearly half a century before the old church was demolished. Work began on the huge new building in 1511. The benefactor

was Sir Henry Trecarrel, a mayor and alderman of the town, who paid for the work after his wife and infant son died. Trecarrel had been rebuilding his own house some 4 miles (6.5km) south of Launceston, but he stopped the work and moved all his men, including a large number of excellent masons and carvers of granite, to the site of the new church. Here, between 1511 and 1524, they erected an extraordinary granite structure that reached 103 feet (31 metres) long. Space was allocated at the western end of the church for a large new tower, but this was never built; houses and then a 'mayoralty room' – now the vestry – were eventually constructed on the site.

Inside the church, the floor is at a lower level than the ground outside, and there are eight bays, with a wider bay for the rood screen at the entrance to the chancel. The arcades are fashioned from granite in the Cornish late Perpendicular style. Almost all the furnishings date, rather surprisingly, from the late 19th and early 20th centuries, including some remarkably fine bench-ends that were installed between 1893 and 1894.

It is, however, the remarkable external granite work that is the glory of Launceston's church. Granite is, of course, an exceptionally hard material, and it must have involved immense effort to carve all the bas-relief work. Masses of carved panels can be seen all around the church. These are partly in a late Perpendicular style, but they are also reminiscent of the early Renaissance with many fruits and flowers carved into the stone, including pomegranates, thistles and the Tudor rose.

The south porch is particularly fine, and contains carvings of St George and St Martin, the coats of arms belonging to the Trecarrels and Kelways (his wife's family) and the date AD 1511. A remarkable sequence of carved letters runs around the outside of the church, with shields forming the gaps between words, which include AVE MARIA GRACIA PLENA. Under the east window of the church, set in a wide niche, is a recumbent figure of St Mary Magdalene and above the window the Royal arms can be seen.

ABOVE: *The detached 14th-century tower is the only surviving remnant of an earlier church on this site. In the foreground is the wonderful south porch.*

RIGHT: *St George and the Dragon are carved in granite on the south porch.*

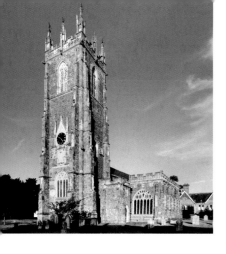

ST ANDREW, CULLOMPTON

DEVON

ABOVE: *The magnificent west tower and Lane Chapel as seen from the south-west.*

BELOW: *The beautiful fan-vault in the Lane Chapel, which was paid for by local cloth merchant John Lane.*

his splendid parish church is situated on the southern side of a lovely little town in eastern Devon. Between the 15th and the 18th centuries the town was an important centre for the cloth trade, which had made some of its families very rich indeed. As a result of this, the whole church was rebuilt in the 16th century. There are some superb features, for example an elaborately decorated 100-foot (30-metre) tall tower, the exceptional fan-vaulted outer chapel and the wonderful high roof that covers the clerestoried nave and chancel.

All trace of an earlier church has disappeared above ground. Once through the tower entrance, the church has a great long nave and chancel with six bays and well-proportioned arcades on either side, which are constructed from Beer stone, a hard chalk from the south-east Devon coast. At the western end there is a large gallery that dates from 1637 and is home to the church's organ. Above all of this is a magnificent boarded high wagon roof. This is supported on small angel brackets and each panel of the roof has cross-ribs on it.

The eastern end of the church is dominated by the vast rood screen and loft, which were repainted and gilded first in the mid-19th century and again more recently. In the early 1840s, the chancel was restored with money given by William Froude (1810–79), the engineer responsible for the Great Western Railway from Somerset to Exeter. The rood loft is coved out on both sides of the screen and has a mass of gilt decoration on it. Amazingly, the carved wooden base of the rood itself – which includes images of the rocks of Golgotha, skulls and crossbones, Mary and John and the mortice holes for the cross – has survived and this is now on show at the western end of the Lane Chapel.

Apart from the two aisles and chapels, there is an extra chapel, on the southern side of the church, which is covered by a magnificent fan-vault, with pendants down the middle. This remarkable addition was paid for by John Lane between 1526 and 1529, and was constructed to serve as his own chantry chapel. Lane was a very wealthy cloth merchant, and he indicated his position for posterity by having his merchant's mark, cloth-shears and teasel-frames

carved on the corbels, along with the instruments of Christ's Passion. These can also be observed on the outside of the chapel on some of the carved buttresses, alongside representations of some of the ships owned by Lane. Sadly, the carvings are somewhat weathered in places, as is the long inscription round the outside of the lower part of the chapel, which asks you to remember the souls of John Lane, his wife, Thomsyn, and their children.

Cullompton's church was being rebuilt right up to the Reformation in 1548, and the last thing to be completed was the impressive tower, which has the arms of Bishop Veysey of Exeter on it. It is built from the local red sandstone, but also has many features on it that are carved in Beer or Ham Hill stone, the most remarkable being the carved rood in the centre. Situated above the west window, this is lucky to have survived the iconoclasm under Edward VI in 1548.

ABOVE: *The impressive rood screen and loft run right across the east end of the church. Note also the great, colourful boarded wagon roof.*

ST MARY, OTTERY ST MARY

DEVON

ABOVE: *An evangelist carved on a panel of the 1772 pulpit.*

BELOW: *The view east from the nave, with the crossing in the foreground.*

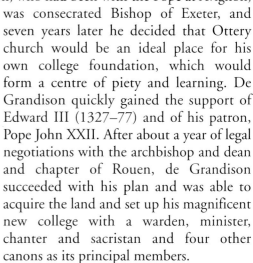

Often known as a 'miniature Exeter cathedral', this is one of the most remarkable parish churches in the whole of south-west England. It is a large but fairly low building on a hill above the market town of Ottery St Mary and the River Otter, about 12 miles (19km) east of Exeter. In 1061, Edward the Confessor (1042–66) gave the manor and parish to the great cathedral of Rouen in Normandy. The shell of the western chancel and transepts of the present great church were probably erected by the dean and chapter of Rouen in the later 13th century.

In 1327, a powerful priest called John de Grandison, who had been with the Pope at Avignon, was consecrated Bishop of Exeter, and seven years later he decided that Ottery church would be an ideal place for his own college foundation, which would form a centre of piety and learning. De Grandison quickly gained the support of Edward III (1327–77) and of his patron, Pope John XXII. After about a year of legal negotiations with the archbishop and dean and chapter of Rouen, de Grandison succeeded with his plan and was able to acquire the land and set up his magnificent new college with a warden, minister, chanter and sacristan and four other canons as its principal members.

Over the next decade or so, de Grandison rebuilt and enlarged the church, using his own cathedral as his model. Most unusually, but as at Exeter, the transepts became low flanking towers and, further east, flanking two-storey vestries were added, which mirror Exeter's eastern transepts. Beyond this, chapels were added at the ends of the choir aisles with a fine new Lady chapel between them. On the western side, a grand, but shorter, aisled nave was added with a series of four ceremonial doorways in the west front. Unlike Exeter Cathedral, the windows at Ottery St Mary are relatively plain, but there are fine vaults throughout the church and some beautifully carved vault-bosses.

The one great addition to the church is the exceptional 'Dorset aisle' on the northern side of the nave. This has a fine outer porch for the parishioners, and inside it is covered with a beautiful fan and pendant vault. It was built in about 1520 by Bishops Oldham and Veysey of Exeter, with Cicely, Countess of Wiltshire as a major patron. On one of the arcade capitals for the aisle is a beautifully carved elephant's head.

The medieval college was dissolved in 1545, and the new governors of the church were first appointed in 1552, a system of administration that still survives. During the 19th and 20th centuries, several major restorations of the church took place, which have not always fitted in with the medieval church. In the south transept, for example, the walls were covered in glazed mosaic tiles in 1878. Most unfortunately, the walls were stripped of plaster in 1919, and the vaults were repainted in very un-medieval colours in 1977.

BELOW: *The church at Ottery St Mary has imposing flanking towers; note also the major 16th-century addition of the 'Dorset aisle' to the left.*

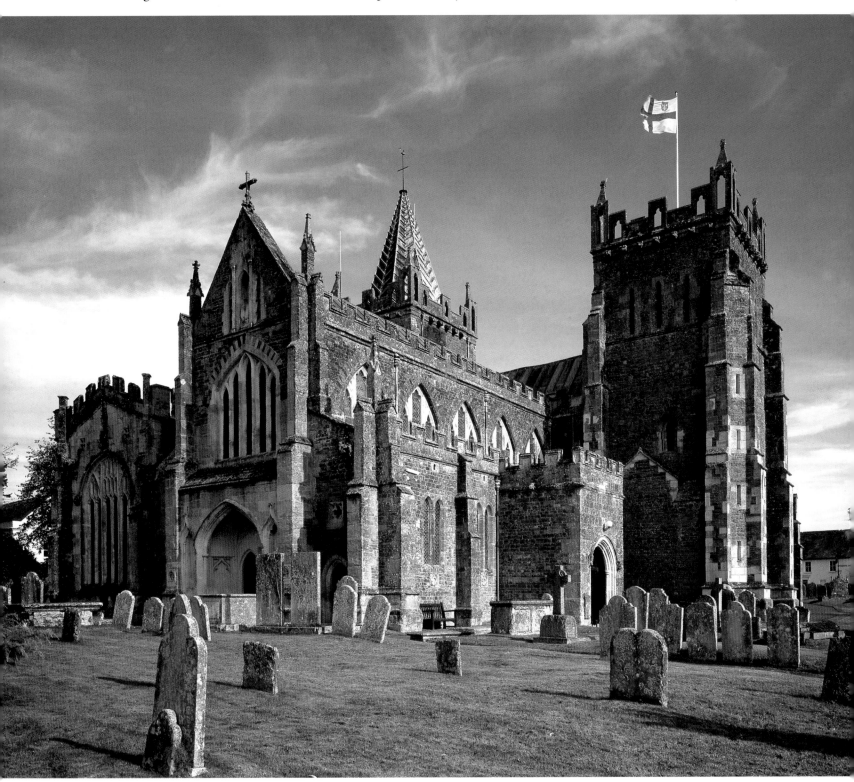

ST WINIFRED, BRANSCOMBE

DEVON

ABOVE: *The monument to Anne Mychell (who died in 1606) can be found in the south transept.*

BELOW: *The church, with its large 12th-century tower, sits protected within a combe.*

his church is beautifully sited in a valley close to the sea on the south-eastern coast of Devon. The unusual dedication suggests that the site is an early one, but whether the saint is the obscure 7th-century St Winifred from North Wales, or St Boniface, who was also known as St Winfred of Crediton, is unknown. When the new cathedral was established at Exeter in 1050, Branscombe was given to the bishop and his canons. It was perhaps Robert of Chichester, the third Norman bishop of Exeter from 1138 to 1155, who built the earliest part of the present church. This consisted of a short nave with a tower to the east of it, beyond which was probably a small sanctuary. The tower over the early chancel area is exceptional because it is a massive three-stage structure with a top parapet on a corbel table, and an original round stair-

turret on the north, which led up to a first-floor chamber and the belfry above. In the 15th century, a new doorway was made from the stair turret to the rood loft, which is no longer there, at the west end of the chancel.

In the late 13th century, Walter of Branscombe, a notable Bishop of Exeter between 1258 and 1280, started the process of rebuilding and enlarging his cathedral from the east end. This bishop, no doubt a native of Branscombe, was also perhaps responsible for enlarging his own parish church, with the addition of transepts and a lengthened nave and south porch. The north and south transepts each had double lancets on their eastern sides, which are now completely blocked up, with a pair of altars beneath them. Only the remains of a double piscina in the north transept survives to prove this.

The final enlargement of the church was the replacement of the small eastern sanctuary by a fine new chancel in the early 14th century. This had a triple sedilia and piscina to the south of the high altar, and small lower shuttered windows (a fairly unusual survival) below the western windows on the north and south sides of the chancel. These were to allow people in the churchyard to see the priest celebrating the mass. In the late 15th century, Bishop Neville had the very fine five-light Perpendicular east window put in; evidence of this is provided by the carving of his coat of arms on the external hood mould.

After the Reformation, a splendid west gallery was put into the nave. A rare external stone staircase to this gallery survives on the south side. The well-known architect W.D. Caroe restored the church in 1911. He left the box pews in the north transept and the fine triple-

decker pulpit next to them in place, and revealed some traces of medieval wall paintings on the walls. The church also contains some fine post-medieval monuments.

ABOVE: *The view east through the tower to the chancel; to the left of the arch is the unusual 18th-century triple-decker pulpit.*

ST GEORGE, DUNSTER

SOMERSET

ABOVE: *Thomas Luttrell (died 1570), High Sheriff of Somerset, and his wife Margaret (née Hadley), lie in a sumptuous tomb in the south aisle.*

BELOW: *Detail of the coved ceiling on the magnificent rood screen, which dates from c. 1498.*

Dunster is a fine market town situated near the north-western coast of Somerset and dominated by its hilltop castle. The castle was first inhabited by the Mohun family in the Norman period. However, they sold it to the Luttrells in 1376. In about 1090, William de Mohun gave the church of Dunster to the Bishop of Bath, John de Villula, so that the monks at Bath could rebuild it and add a Benedictine priory alongside. This was always a fairly small house and virtually nothing of it survives today; it was dissolved in 1535. The so-called 'cloister', barn and fine circular dovecote to the north all date from after 1535.

In the church, however, the massive piers of the crossing tower are clearly Norman and there are attached columns and capitals on the western side that date from the same period. The western doorway of the nave is of the late 12th century, although it was almost completely rebuilt and re-carved in the 19th century. There were also early north and south transepts, but these were totally rebuilt in the late Middle Ages.

The eastern arm of the church, which was quite heavily restored by G.E. Street (1824–81) between 1875 and 1877, was rebuilt with flanking chapels in the 13th century and contained the monks' choir. There is also a rather unusual 13th-century arch between the south

transept and south-eastern Luttrell Chapel, which was widened out below in the early 16th century.

One very rare survival is an original document, which dates from 1442 and forms a contract between the parishioners and a mason, John Marys, who was charged with rebuilding the upper part of the tower. All the details of the tower are carefully specified, and they include the three diagonal buttresses (called 'French' buttresses) and the 'vice' (stair-turret) in the 'fowrth pyler', as well the details of the windows, including those in the 'bell bedd' (belfry). There was also to be a 'batylment' on top with four 'pynacles', the 'fowrth pynacle standing upon the vice after reson and gode proportion'. All the work was to be completed within three years, and there can be no doubt that the existing tower at Dunster was built between 1442 and 1445, as specified in the document.

Sometime after this, the parishioners rebuilt the nave and aisles, although the north aisle was curtailed by a priory building to the north-west. In 1498, there was a demarcation dispute between the monks and the parishioners, and this led to a written arbitration at Glastonbury. As a result, the parish had to construct its own chancel at the east end of the nave, and the magnificent rood screen still runs right across the church, defining the boundary between the nave and chancel in the 'new' parish church. Almost all that now survives of the fabric of the nave and aisles dates from the years around 1498.

The porch and beautiful three-light Perpendicular windows present a splendid crenellated façade to the town on the south side. A major element of this façade is the crenellated stair-turret, which led to the rood loft. Ironically, there is no longer a vice in the turret, only a 'cupboard' with a tiny Victorian fireplace!

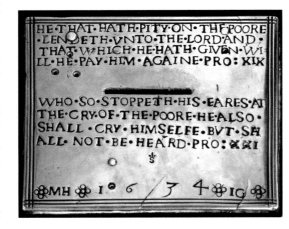

ST MARY, STOGUMBER

SOMERSET

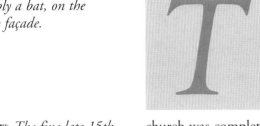

This parish on the edge of the Quantocks takes its unusual name from a corruption of one of the commonest names, Stoke, and that of one of the Anglo-Saxon owners of the manor, Gumer or Gunner. There was certainly an earlier church here, but the earliest visible element is the 14th-century Old Red Sandstone tower at the south-west corner of the church, which has a crenellated south porch attached to it. The western part of the south arcade, the south aisle wall and the shell of the south-east chantry chapel also date from the 14th century; the rest of the church was completely rebuilt in the 15th and early 16th centuries, and the chancel was rebuilt in the late 19th century.

The majority of the rebuilding took place in the late 15th century when the nave was demolished and replaced with arcades, well-carved capitals, and a new double-gabled wall on the west.

RIGHT: *Arts and Crafts stencilled decoration from the late 19th century can be found on the north side of the chancel.*

BELOW: *The fine tomb of Sir George Sydenham, who lies between his successive wives, is on the south side of the chancel.*

A new stone pulpit was also added. The north side of the church faces into the village, and here a grand crenellated façade to the aisle was built, with a very tall double-gabled porch in the centre, which, surprisingly, does not have an upper chamber, but a high roof nevertheless. At the eastern end of this aisle is another chantry chapel with an unusual double arcade to the chancel and a low recessed tomb set in the north wall. Fixed in it is a later brass dedicated to Elizabeth Windham, who died in 1585. All the 15th-century work in the nave and aisles is covered with fine wagon-roofs that date from the same period, although it is a pity that the lath-and-plaster ceilings are no longer present.

On the south side of the chancel is the large classical tomb of Sir George Sydenham – his name is written Sr. Gorge Sidnum on the tomb, so spelling clearly did not matter in 1589, the year in which he died! The tomb has a monumental canopy with large coffered arches and three pairs of Corinthian columns on either side. Lying within is Sir George's effigy with his two wives tucked in below him on either side. The Sydenhams lived at Combe Sydenham, just west of Stogumber, and Sir George's daughter, Elizabeth, married the Elizabethan adventurer Sir Francis Drake. The south-east chantry became the Sydenham family chapel, and is still a private chapel screened by railings.

From the outside, it is clear that the east wall of the chancel was totally rebuilt in the 19th century, but it is only within the building that one can see what a splendid and unusual restoration was carried out by a Victorian vicar, the Reverend Edward Jones, who was incumbent here from 1871 to 1907. At the beginning of his incumbency Jones spent £4,200 on completely remodelling the chancel. The work was finished by May 1875, when the Bishop of Bath and Wells re-dedicated it, and we now have Jones's finely tiled floor and beautifully painted and stencilled ceilings and walls in the style of the leader of the Arts and Crafts movement, William Morris.

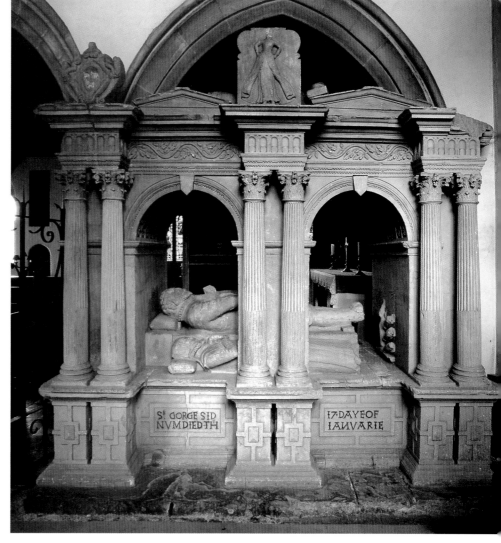

ST MARY MAGDALENE, TAUNTON

SOMERSET

ABOVE: *This angel harpist can be found on the chancel vault.*

ABOVE: *This angel harpist can be found on the chancel vault.*

OPPOSITE: *From the west end there is a breathtaking view of the very fine medieval masonry and spectacular angel roof of the nave, with the chancel beyond.*

BELOW: *One of the repainted and gilded angels on the nave roof.*

Taunton had an Anglo-Saxon monastery from the 8th century, but it was the acquisition of the great manor of Taunton Dene by the bishops of Winchester in the 10th century that gave it an important castle and town. On the site of the church of St Mary Magdalene was an Anglo-Saxon and Norman church, and fragments of the plans of this building were found during the late 19th-century restoration. The church was transformed into an Augustinian priory in the early 12th century. The brother of King Stephen (1135–54), Henry of Blois (1100–1171), who was Abbot of Glastonbury and Bishop of Winchester for many years, moved the priory to the north-east side of the town so that he could enlarge the castle. A new parish church was then built, although only the 13th-century arcade to the north aisle survives from this building. The rest of the church was rebuilt in the 15th and early 16th centuries, at a time when Taunton was a very rich cloth town, and the double aisles on either side of the nave show how the exceptional size of the population needed to be accommodated in the church. Taunton also has another fine urban parish church, dedicated to St James, which is situated not far to the north of St Mary Magdalene.

Inside the church, the view east from the middle of the nave shows the fine architecture of the late 15th century at its best. First, there are the slender arcades with capitals covered in angels, above which are very large traceried clerestory windows. Between each of the windows are statue

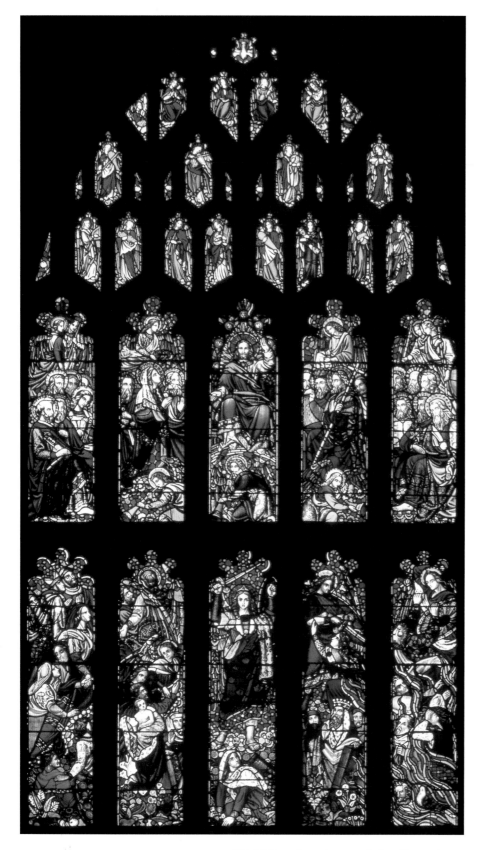

ABOVE: *High Victorian glass made by Alexander Gibbs in 1862–4 appears in the west window.*

ABOVE RIGHT: *The great west tower, the church's most impressive feature, as seen from the south side of the chancel.*

niches, which contain 19th-century statues, and above all this is a wonderful roof. The angels and other details were gilded for the first time in 1968, making the roof even more striking.

The great glory of the church, however, is the really magnificent 163-foot (50-metre) high great west tower. Somerset has many fine bell-towers, but this is surely the finest and most beautiful, as well as being the largest. It was built in the years around 1500, but amazingly it was taken down and completely rebuilt between 1852 and 1862, using much of its original masonry. Ham Hill stone was used for the main dressings, with ashlar and local red sandstone for the rest. The tower has three full storeys of double windows, each displaying Somerset tracery, above the even larger west window. The top storey is slightly set back and has additional blank panelling above the extra large belfry openings. The whole structure culminates in very large pierced crenellations with even larger pierced pinnacles and crocketed spirelets at the corners. The lowest storey is covered in statue niches around the west portal and window.

The final addition to the church was the two-storey south porch and its associated masonry of the western half of the south aisle. The porch actually has the date 'Anno 1508' on it, a high point in Taunton just before the Reformation.

ST MARY, ISLE ABBOTS

SOMERSET

sle Abbots is a fairly remote village that takes its name from the River Isle, and is situated just beyond the south-western corner of the Somerset Levels. In the Middle Ages it belonged to the Abbey of Muchelney, which is only 6 miles (10km) away to the north-east, and the very fine parish church has one of the most splendid of all Somerset towers.

No sign of an earlier church remains, but the chancel was rebuilt by the abbey in the later 13th century and it retains its excellent windows, a stepped five-light east window and four beautiful three-light side windows with foiled circles above. On the south side of the chancel is an exceptionally fine piscina, which is set in beautiful panelling. To the west is a remarkable sedilia, which has three curve-backed seats. Its canopies were apparently removed in the early 14th century, when plainer back panelling was installed. The nave was perhaps rebuilt a little later, but it still has a 13th-century south door, with early 14th-century windows on either side. There must have been a 13th-century south porch, but it was rebuilt in a splendid fashion in the early 16th century with beautiful pierced crenellations filled with carved quatrefoils. Inside the porch, a remarkable stone

ABOVE: *A 'hunky punk', as such grotesques are known in Somerset, blows a bagpipe on the north-west corner of the tower.*

BELOW: *The south-east corner of the chancel has an exceptional piscina and equally fine sedilia.*

fan-vault with a central pendant was installed.

A beautiful north aisle and an eastern Lady chapel were also added in the 16th century. The chapel and the nave still contain many bench-ends from the original pews, although the seats were remade in the 19th century. The north arcade has fine flat four-centred arches and there are also six beautiful late Perpendicular windows, also with fine four-centred heads, and a wooden roof. The aisle also contains a late Norman font, the bowl of which appears to have been partially re-carved a century or so after it was first made. Nearby is another rare survival, a working barrel organ, which was made in about 1835 and can play about forty tunes.

All the carved masonry in the church is made from golden Ham Hill stone, the quarries for which are about 8 miles (13km) to the east of the church. The best use of all for this stone is the magnificent 81-foot (25-metre) high west tower. It is a superbly designed structure, which still – amazingly – retains almost all its medieval statues, each of which is held up by an angel and housed within a niche. Only the two lowest statues on the west face are missing, but above are four statues, which depict Christ rising, the Virgin and Child, and St Peter and St Paul. On the south side are three statues, with two on the east face and one on the north, where the turret takes up much of the space. The many pinnacles and windows are filled with Somerset tracery and the set-back buttresses and beautiful pierced and crenellated parapets all come together to form an exceptional structure.

ABOVE AND BELOW: *These statues of Christ rising from the dead and of the Virgin and Child are found on the west front.*

RIGHT: *St Mary's has a truly magnificent west tower, made from local Ham Hill stone, which abounds with almost all its original medieval statues.*

ST BARTHOLOMEW, CREWKERNE

SOMERSET

This very large and well-lit parish church is situated in the southernmost part of Somerset. It a very good example of the late Perpendicular style of Gothic architecture of the 15th and early 16th centuries, when the small town of Crewkerne was extremely wealthy due to its involvement in the textile and wool trades. Long before this, however, there must have been a major Anglo-Saxon minster church here, and the land attached to it was an extensive royal estate. After the Norman Conquest, William the Conqueror gave Crewkerne's estate and church to his personal Abbey of St Stephen at Caen in Normandy, the great church in which William was buried and which still stands today, having miraculously survived the destruction of the Second World War.

After the Norman Conquest, the church at Crewkerne was almost certainly rebuilt around a large crossing tower. Although this tower does not survive above ground, one can see in the present crossing area a series of breaks and changes in the masonry that indicate the various stages of rebuilding around the tower during the late Middle Ages. For all this work beautiful golden-brown Ham Hill stone was used.

The various large areas of space inside the eastern half of the church relate to a series of chantry chapels that were built here for the richest of the parishioners. In the slightly earlier south transept, a pair of chapels, one of which is now taken up by the organ, are relatively modest in size, but on the north are two much longer chapels. These chapels were probably all built in the early 16th century, although, sadly, detailed documentary evidence for them does not survive.

The very fine nave, which is almost square in plan, was probably completely rebuilt in the 1480s and 1490s with a clerestory. It may have been designed by William Smyth, the master mason of Wells Cathedral, and the west front reminds one of the grand west fronts of Bath Abbey

ABOVE: *This 15th-century angel corbel supports the nave roof.*

BELOW: *The carved reredos behind the high altar was made in 1903.*

and St George's Chapel at Windsor Castle. At Windsor, the crossing tower was never finished, but at Crewkerne a fine battlemented crossing tower exists. Crenellated battlements were also added all round the outside of the church.

One of the unique features of the church is the covered 'seat' behind a grating on the outside south-east corner of the south transept. It was almost certainly made to hold a large image of a saint.

LEFT: *A stunning horizontal reed stop made from burnished copper was installed on the organ below the large west window in 2004 and creates a superlative sound.*

BELOW: *St Bartholomew's church is a fine example of the Perpendicular style in the golden-coloured Ham Hill stone; it has a beautifully proportioned west front and south porch.*

ST NICHOLAS, STUDLAND

DORSET

T his magnificent and very sturdy early Norman church is situated below the great chalk promontory on the north side of the Isle of Purbeck. It is set back from beautiful Studland Bay, and its parish runs north over the barren heathland to Poole Harbour. On this shore, 2½ miles (4km) north-west of the church, King Edward I (1272–1307) founded Newtown in 1286, which he hoped would rival Poole; however, the settlement quickly failed.

In the Domesday Book, Studland was one of several manors in Dorset held by Robert, Count of Mortain, who was William the Conqueror's half-brother. Robert was a powerful man and he may have initiated the building of the church here, as, despite some earlier

ABOVE: *A Janus-like double-headed corbel on the nave.*

BELOW: *The massive early 12th-century tower remains unfinished in the 21st century.*

ABOVE: *An early 12th-century carved cushion capital on the south side of the old chancel arch, and a corbel with copulating figures on the south porch.*

ABOVE RIGHT: *The tower arches suffer from distorted masonry and may be the reason behind the unfinished tower.*

accounts, there is no evidence for an Anglo-Saxon church on the site.

The large nave is a well-preserved and typical early Norman church of the late 11th century. It has centrally placed north and south doorways, which are flanked high up by small early-Norman round-headed windows, which on the south and west were enlarged in the 18th century. The most notable feature of the nave, however, is the carved corbel-table, which runs all the way round the top of the walls, just below the eaves. Here we can see some splendid grotesque carvings of human and animal figures, which, like prehistoric carving, can be interpreted in any way you choose.

Not long after the nave was built, probably at the beginning of the 12th century, the original eastern end of the church was demolished and a remarkable tower and eastern sanctuary were built. These had massive walls and, most exceptionally, large quadripartite rib-vaults. Great

moulded arches were also erected between the nave and tower where the modern choir stalls are placed and between the tower and sanctuary. Both these arches have spread at the top and begun to collapse, so they are now held together by ugly but strong iron ties. The movement in the structure may have been the reason why the great bell-tower was never completed. It is now covered, as are the nave and sanctuary, by a fine roof fashioned in local Purbeck slate.

In the 13th century, a large three-light east window was put in, but otherwise little further work was carried out on the main structure of the church, apart from the enlargement of the windows and the addition of a porch after the Reformation. This was, no doubt, due to the relative poverty of the parish in the later Middle Ages.

In 1975–6, a modern 'Anglo-Saxon' cross was carved by Treleven Haysom, who comes from a local family of masons. It is placed beside the road leading up to the church on the south.

ST NICHOLAS, MORETON

DORSET

eside the River Frome, a few miles east of Dorchester, is a remarkable Georgian parish church, which is more like a family church. This is because it lies on a mound just inside the park of Moreton House, which has been the family home of the Framptons since the 14th century. There was a medieval parish church on this site, dedicated first to St Magnus the Martyr and then to St Nicholas of Myra (a place in modern Turkey), but the present church was completely rebuilt by James Frampton in 1776, having first rebuilt the nearby Moreton House between 1742 and 1745.

The new church just had a large, open nave and apsidal sanctuary and was made with brick and faced in fine Portland stone ashlar. On the south side is what appears to be an aisle, although

ABOVE: *The grave of 'Lawrence of Arabia' lies in Moreton's detached cemetery.*

BELOW: *Whistler's engraved glass and the simple, pale-coloured interior makes St Nicholas's chancel light and open.*

41

it is actually a tower porch, which is flanked by the pews of the Framptons. To the south-east, facing the eastern side of the church, was the family pew. This encloses a fireplace and the walls around it are covered in family memorials. On the south-west – and without a fireplace – was the servants' pew, which is now the vestry.

In 1840, another member of the family, the Reverend William Frampton, became rector of the church and remained there until his death fifty-eight years later. In the first few years of his incumbency, £5,000 was spent on rebuilding the church. A new north aisle was added in 1841, which was followed by a series of ribbed ceilings in plaster. In 1847–78, the timber vaulting shafts were replaced in stone, after which a whole series of new fittings were installed, including the font and surviving encaustic floor tiles. A new west porch and doorway were added in 1848 to replace the earlier parishioners' north doorway.

On 8 October 1940, during the Second World War, a stray bomb blew out much of the church's north wall, devastating the interior. The fine 19th-century windows, which had been designed by Thomas Willement (1786–1871), were destroyed. Ten years later the church was rebuilt. The distinguished architectural historian Sir Howard Colvin made the inspired suggestion to replace the semi-opaque glass windows with clear glass, on which engraved drawings should be etched by the wonderful artist, Laurence Whistler (1912–2000). The first set of windows was installed in the apse in 1955, and it was followed by the rest of the windows over the next 30 years. There are many beautifully engraved images, most depicting the effects of light, and in the Trinity Chapel window there is even an aerial view of the building's mother church – Salisbury Cathedral, where more of Whistler's engraved glass can be seen.

In a detached cemetery, which is not far from the church, is the grave of T.E. Lawrence – 'Lawrence of Arabia' – who was killed nearby on his motorbike on 10 May 1935.

BELOW: *The Trinity chapel window of 1982 features Salisbury Cathedral at the bottom of the centre light.*

BELOW RIGHT: *The space for the family pews stands prominently to the left of the church, when seen from the south-east.*

ST JOHN THE BAPTIST, BERE REGIS

DORSET

he little town of Bere Regis in east Dorset was made a 'free borough' by Edward I, hence its grand name. The church lies on the south-east side of the town, just above the watercress beds of the Milborne Brook, and from the north it appears to be largely late medieval. The fine late Perpendicular west tower and the chequer-work masonry all suggest a date of around 1500, and on entering the church its magnificent nave roof can be viewed, which dates from the same period.

The earliest part of the fabric, however, is the masonry on the north-east and east sides of the nave, which probably date from the later 11th century – the first church on the site is referred to in the Domesday Book, which was completed in 1086. By about 1160, the population had increased, and aisles were added to the nave, which was still quite small. The capitals of this date have some fine carved heads on them at the angles. The population had expanded by the time that Bere Regis was created a free borough at the end of the 13th century, as the nave had been lengthened westwards and supported by two large arches. By this time, the chancel had also been rebuilt with a fine new three-light east window.

The south aisle, with a Lady chapel to the east, was rebuilt in the early 14th century by the Turberville family, who were lords of the manor and had a house just to the east of the church. Although early 14th-century windows with reticulated tracery survive, there was much rebuilding of this aisle after a fire in 1760. The very fine five-light window on the south side of the Turberville chapel, which has carved jambs, was installed in 1535, as requested in John Turberville's will.

Between 1486 and 1500, John Morton (c. 1420–1500), whose mother was a Turberville and who was born in the parish, was Archbishop of Canterbury and Chancellor of England – he was also made a cardinal in 1493 by the infamous and corrupt Pope Alexander VI, also known as Rodrigo Borgia.

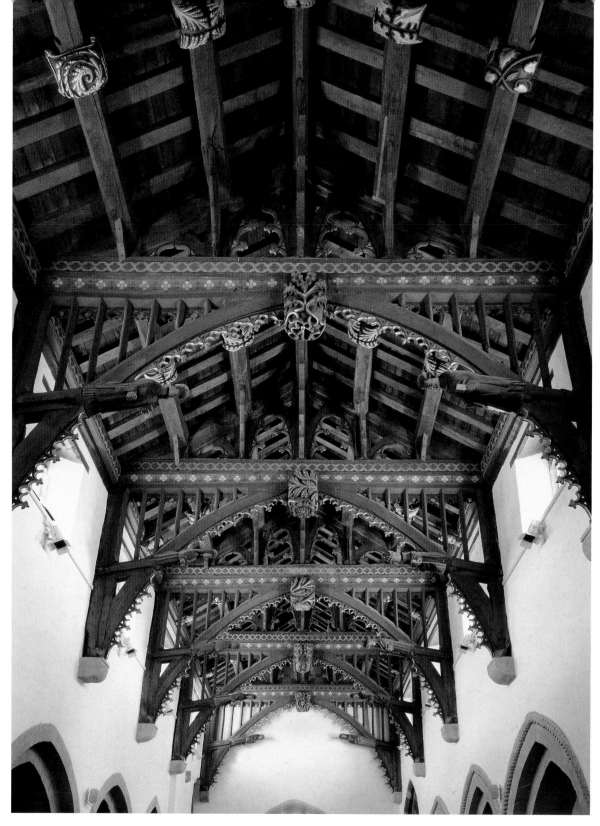

Morton is said to have paid for the rebuilding of the upper walls of the nave, the clerestory and the really magnificent arch-braced roof. This splendid and elaborate piece of work, with much cusping and large central bosses, has a series of twelve apostles attached to the hammer beams, some of which are represented with their attributes; for example Judas is seen with his money bag. The chancel was also rebuilt in the late 15th century. In his will, Cardinal Morton founded a chantry in the church. This was at the east end of the north aisle and is now rather cut off by the organ. Of the same date was a rood screen, which is now gone. The stair to the rood loft and a large squint to the chancel can be seen in the Morton Chapel.

Post-Reformation monuments in the south aisle and the 18th-century burial vault beneath it continued to commemorate the Turbervilles, and the various successions to the manor are recorded in the stained glass of the south window.

ST CUTHBURGA, WIMBORNE MINSTER

DORSET

In the middle of the Anglo-Saxon period Wimborne Minster was an important royal centre. A double monastery, which housed men and women in separate buildings, was established here before the end of the 7th century, and by AD 705, Cuthburh, the sister of King Ine of Wessex (688–726), was the abbess. After her death in about 725, Cuthburh's tomb became an important shrine, and in 871 the body of Ethelred, the elder brother of King Alfred (871–99), was brought here for burial.

Just before the Norman Conquest in 1066, Edward the Confessor established a new collegiate church here – the earlier church seems to have been destroyed during a Viking raid, although fragments of the masonry of this building probably survive in the crossing area. From the early 12th century, this cruciform church was rebuilt and greatly enlarged and its crossing arches date from this period. By the late 12th century, the nave and chancel had both acquired aisles, and the fine Romanesque arcades of this date are best viewed in the nave. At the same time, the upper stages of the crossing tower were built, using quite large quantities of a local ironstone known as heathstone.

BELOW: *The view eastwards to the crossing and raised sanctuary. Note the early pointed Romanesque arches in the nave.*

In the early 13th century, the college of canons at Wimborne was re-organized under the dean and a proper choir was created with a fine new chancel beyond. In 1318, King Edward II (1307–27) made Wimborne a 'free chapel' and 'Royal Peculiar', which meant that the church was answerable only to the monarchy, as Westminster Abbey still is today. The church was extended to the west and large new chapels were constructed on either side of the chancel. A stone spire was added to the crossing tower, but sadly this fell in 1600. Under the sanctuary, a fine vaulted crypt was installed and a vaulted treasury was created on the south side of the chancel. Above this treasury, now the choir vestry, is Wimborne's famous chained library, which was created in 1686.

By the mid-14th century, Wimborne Minster had reached its climax as both a building and an important establishment. The people's part of the building – the nave – was then given a new clerestory in the 15th century, and a large western tower was also added. The chancel also acquired added status, as the fine tombs of John Beaufort, Duke of Somerset, and his wife were placed here in 1444. Beaufort was the grandson of John of Gaunt (1340–99) and the grandfather of King Henry VII. In 1496, Lady Margaret Beaufort (1443–1509), Henry VII's mother, founded a grammar school at the church.

The college was dissolved in 1547, but Wimborne continued as a fine parish church and it retained its status as a Royal Peculiar until 1846. Unfortunately, the eastern arm was rebuilt and over-restored in 1855, but despite this it remains one of the finest parish churches in Dorset.

LEFT: *From the south side of the church, which is made from a mix of Dorset limestone and a darker ironstone, one can see the top-heavy crossing tower. The church once had an elegant spire instead of today's massive parapet and pinnacles.*

ST MARY, BREAMORE

HAMPSHIRE

This remarkably complete church, which is largely Anglo-Saxon, was only 'discovered' as such during a major restoration in 1897. It is now one of the best-preserved churches of its period in southern England, despite being cut down and remodelled to a certain extent in the 15th century.

The church was first built in the early 11th century and was originally over 100 feet (30 metres) long. Unfortunately, we do not know who built the church, but it was perhaps for a royal manor. Local flint and some re-used Roman material were used, and the large blocks for the quoins, jambs and 'long and short' pilasters were primarily made with newly quarried Hurdcott stone – a form of Upper Greensand – and transported 13 miles (20km) along the Avon Valley from just west of Wilton. Some local ironstone was also used.

In plan, the church has a sizeable crossing area with a large nave to the west and a small sanctuary to the east. To the north and south were transepts. The northern transept, or *porticus* in Latin, was destroyed in the 15th century; the southern transept was left intact and still retains two original windows and the original doorway into the crossing, above which is a very prominent Anglo-Saxon inscription. Two more of the original windows survive high up in the north wall of the nave, and one can suggest that there were originally four on each side. The west wall of the nave was also rebuilt in the 15th century, after an Anglo-Saxon chamber was demolished.

ABOVE: *A mutilated Anglo-Saxon rood sits above the nave's south doorway.*

BELOW, LEFT: *The monumental inscription on the Anglo-Saxon arch says: 'Here is manifested the Word to thee'.*

BELOW: *This corbelled head of an anxious man is on the south side of the west tower arch.*

It may originally have contained the main doorway into the church with a large carved rood above it inside. This was taken down and placed above the south doorway to the nave in the 15th century, although sadly it was badly mutilated during the Reformation.

In the 12th century, St Mary's became the parish church, and a fine Norman south porch and doorway into the nave were built. After the Anglo-Saxon rood was put above the Norman south doorway, a new upper chamber was made over the porch, with the rood as its centrepiece. The walls were painted with various scenes and an altar was placed on the east side. The floor to this upper chamber was removed in 1897, so that one can now stand in the porch and look up at the rather decayed paintings and mutilated rood. On the north the outlines of the figures of Jesus on the Cross with Mary and John below can still be seen with the remains of a painted landscape behind. The south side, much more decayed, has the unusual scene of Judas hanging from a tree.

The other major changes to the church involved lowering the walls of the chancel in the 14th century and installing a southern doorway and new east window. The roof over the crossing was remodelled in the 15th century as a belfry. The bells are rung from the floor of the choir.

BELOW: *From the south-east the Anglo-Saxon south* porticus *and Norman porch can be seen on the left.*

ALL SAINTS, EAST MEON

HAMPSHIRE

The manor of East Meon belonged to the bishops of Winchester. The late medieval Court House (the name for the manor house) still survives, just to the south-east of the church. Dominating both, however, is the rounded shape of Park Hill, which lies immediately to the north of the church in the medieval deer-park and towers over the north side of the church.

There must have been an Anglo-Saxon church here, but the present building dates from the mid-12th century and was almost certainly erected in the time of the very powerful Bishop Henry of Blois, who was the half-brother of King Stephen (1135–54). The church Henry constructed was cruciform, and particularly fine is the crossing tower with triple openings in each face for the belfry. All of the openings are covered in Romanesque decoration, such as scalloped capitals and zig-zag arches. Above this are three circular openings. The tower is low, and capped off with a lead-covered broach-spire, which dates from the late Middle Ages. Of the same date as the spire are the western and southern doorways of the church. The latter was reset in the south aisle wall in the 13th century. These doors also have zig-zag decoration.

The masonry is a mixture of local stone, such as Lower Greensand, and stone from further afield, for example Quarr stone from the Isle of Wight. Inside the church is its greatest treasure, a magnificent font fashioned from black polished marble from Tournai on the Franco–Belgian border. The font dates from the mid-12th century and is covered with dragons, birds, animals and the story of Adam and Eve. It is one of a small number of similar fonts (another is in Winchester Cathedral) that Bishop Henry had brought to England.

In the early 13th century, a south aisle to the nave and a new chapel on the south side of the chancel were built. The south aisle still has its fine arcade and plate tracery windows. After this no further expansion took place, but various new windows were put in during the period of Prior Hinton, who was head of Winchester Cathedral Priory between 1470 and 1498. His arms are outside the windows.

The church underwent some major restoration in 1869–70 and it was re-furnished by Sir Ninian Comper in the early 20th century, who also put in the stained glass of the east window. The most recent addition, of the year 2000, is hidden away on the north side of the nave.

ABOVE: *Made from Tournai marble, the font dates from the 12th century. Here, Eve is shown being tempted by the serpent to eat the apple.*

BELOW: *The south aisle is in the early Gothic style, while the nave is Norman.*

FOLLOWING PAGE: *The modern north extension is visible to the left of the church from the south-west, while Park Hill rises behind.*

ST MARY, BRADING

ISLE OF WIGHT

T he Isle of Wight was one of the last places in England to embrace Christianity. Bishop Wilfrid came here to convert the inhabitants in AD 686. By the early 8th century, the island was part of the diocese of Winchester, and a series of churches had been constructed at the main manors across the middle of the island by the 11th century. One of the most important of these was at Brading at the east end of the island. Here a major settlement grew up around a large natural harbour, which extended from Sandown on the south to St Helen's on the north (most of the haven was finally drained in the 19th century, leaving only the small modern Bembridge harbour).

By the late 12th century, the population of Brading had greatly expanded, as evidenced by the five bays of late Romanesque piers, which have early pointed arches above, on either side of the nave. The nave was completed in about 1200, after which a western tower and stone spire were added, forming a remarkable landmark across Brading Haven. The new tower blocked the gap between the west end of the nave and the main road, so it had to be built with open arches under it to allow medieval processions to pass round the outside of the church while remaining on consecrated ground. Just to the north of the tower, the west wall of the north aisle, which contains a single lancet window, shows the original form of the aisle, as well as the enlarged and rebuilt 15th-century outer wall.

At the eastern ends of the two aisles, family chantry chapels were built in the later Middle Ages. On the north was the De Aula chapel, with 14th-century arches opening into the chancel and north aisle and an outer wall that was

ABOVE: *A wooden effigy of Sir John Oglander (died 1655), a local man and friend of Charles I.*

RIGHT: *On the north side of the Oglander chapel are Oliver Oglander's decoratively carved tomb (c. 1530) and the simple tomb with impressive effigy of Sir John Oglander.*

ABOVE: *The Oglander chapel, seen here in the foreground, was added to the south-east corner of the Norman church in the 14th century.*

BELOW: *The memorial of 1875 to Elizabeth Rollo in the north aisle is typical Victorian mawkishness.*

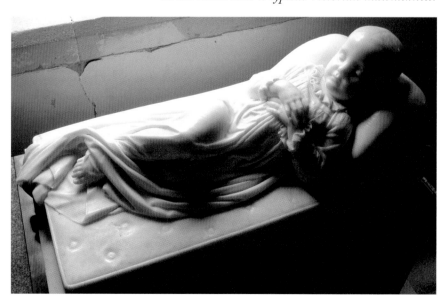

rebuilt in the 15th century. To the south of the chancel, which had its east wall demolished and moved outwards between 1864 and 1866, is the splendid Oglander chapel.

The Oglander family came to the Isle of Wight from Normandy's Cotentin Peninsula in the late 11th century, and owned the manor of Nunwell just west of Brading from the Middle Ages until the 20th century. The chapel is full of heraldry, monuments and memorials to members of the family, which date from the 15th to the 19th century. The most spectacular objects are two late medieval tomb-chests on either side of the chapel, which are the resting places of John Oglander, who died in 1482, and his son, Oliver, who died in 1530. Beyond these are the wonderful French oak effigies of Sir William Oglander, who died in 1608, and Sir John Oglander, who died in 1655. Sir John was a friend of King Charles I (1625–49), and he kept a well-known diary of events at the end of the Civil War. Charles I spent his last night of freedom at the Oglanders' nearby house of Nunwell in 1647, a visit that is described in detail in his friend's diary.

ST THOMAS THE MARTYR, SALISBURY

WILTSHIRE

ABOVE: *An inscribed capital in the south arcade, which dates from c. 1470.*

BELOW: *The leaning south tower porch makes an impressive impact on those viewing the church from the south-west.*

S alisbury, or 'New Sarum', came into existence as a completely new town at the beginning of the 13th century. By the end of the Middle Ages Salisbury had proved very successful, becoming the seventh largest and richest town in England. At its heart, next to the large central market-place, a new church was built in about 1230 and dedicated to St Thomas the Martyr, better known as Archbishop Thomas Becket (1118–1170). After the Reformation the dedication was changed to St Thomas the Apostle. The small size of the original church is probably related to the fact that it was erected at the very same time as the new cathedral was being constructed a short distance to the south.

In 1363, the income of the church, by now a considerable sum, was appropriated by the dean and chapter for the repair of the cathedral's tower and spire, which had been built only half a century before. In return, the cathedral authorities started to rebuild the church, a project that was greatly assisted by the wealthy citizens of Salisbury. The splendid nave aisles and tower porch on the south were erected in the early 15th century and a large body of priests were brought in to serve the church's many chantries. The bell-tower on the south was intended to have a stone spire like the neighbouring cathedral, but when it began to lean to the south – the incline is still visible today – construction was abandoned and the tower was capped with a timber roof.

In 1447, the chancel collapsed, but once again the wealthiest citizens banded

53

together with the cathedral and agreed to pay for an even longer chancel to be built, which was flanked by two larger chantry chapels and a house for the priests on the north. A series of documents record this rebuilding and describe how a major dispute arose between the two wealthiest citizens over the work in 1465. One of these men was the mayor, John Halle. He incited a riotous assembly to pull down the clergy house on the north, which was being built by his rival William Swayne, an affluent wool merchant who had the support of the bishop. Nevertheless, this building (now the vestry) still survives.

The magnificent new eastern arm of the church, with a clerestory to the chancel and fine carved corbels of angels playing musical instruments for the roof posts, was complete by the 1470s. At this point, work started to rebuild the arcades in the nave. Very slender columns were put in, which supported the thinned-down upper wall that contained large clerestory windows. This was a technical advance and allowed more light to come into the nave. Above all this is a fine angel roof, which is still covered in much of its original colour. Unfortunately, only the eastern bay of the nave has so far been cleaned to reveal this – the rest is covered in brown varnish that dates from the 19th century.

In the north-east chapel is a large organ, which was given to Salisbury Cathedral by George III (1760–1820) in 1792. It was brought to the church in 1877, although it is really too large for the building. It could one day be replaced by a new organ in a gallery on the western side of the nave, which is where it stood in the 18th century.

The famous late 15th-century Doom painting over the chancel arch depicts the Last Judgement.

ABOVE: *The nave is light and airy thanks to the slender arches and clerestory windows above. The Doom painting can be seen over the chancel arch.*

OPPOSITE: *These details from the Doom painting show Christ on the rainbow, flanked by the Virgin and St John with the heads of the saints beneath (above); and the damned descending into Hell – note the alewife in the top left corner (below).*

ST MARY, ST KATHARINE AND ALL SAINTS, EDINGTON

WILTSHIRE

dington lies just beyond the northern edge of Salisbury Plain. The village's most famous son, William of Edington, who was Bishop of Winchester between 1345 and 1366, built a remarkable new church in the years after the Black Death of 1348–9. An earlier church on the site was built and owned by the great Benedictine nunnery at Romsey in Hampshire, but in 1351 the bishop, who by this time was immensely wealthy, struck a deal with Romsey Abbey. He agreed to found a new college at Edington for a warden and six priests and completely rebuild the church. In this he was following his master, King Edward III, who set up the College of St George in 1348 at Windsor Castle. Work on Edington's new church began in 1352, but six years later, on 6 April 1358, the bishop decided, perhaps on the suggestion of Edward of Woodstock, the Black Prince, to transform the new foundation. He decided to make it a religious house of the order of Bonhommes, an unusual branch of Augustinian canons.

In its new form as the 'rector and brethren of the convent of Edington' the college had up to eighteen members, who had their own stalls in the chancel. Three years later, when the new church was complete, it was dedicated by Bishop Wyville of Salisbury. With both the bishops of Salisbury and Winchester present, the dedication ceremony must have been a splendid occasion; it was almost certainly at this point that the very rare brass consecration crosses were fixed on the outside and inside walls. The brasses that can be seen today date from a later period.

The church shows the earliest form of Perpendicular architecture at its best. The building is 150 feet (45 metres) long and has an aisled nave, which was built for the parishioners; transepts with chapels and a crossing tower; and an exceptionally fine chancel for the brethren. There is also a grand three-storey porch on the south side of the nave, and to the north the cloister and domestic accommodation would have once stood. The west front, with its double doorway and great window, is particularly striking. It is worth noting that the bishop who built this church also started to rebuild the west front of his vast cathedral at Winchester in the same style.

Inside, there is a sharp contrast between the fine, plain Perpendicular architecture of the aisled nave and the more elaborate decoration beyond the screen, which includes large carved statue niches in the chancel. The windows here are also much larger, though the plaster ceiling, which was put up in about 1790, gives the chancel a strange 'cover'. The plaster ceilings in the nave and transepts were made in 1663. Most of the fittings in the church date from after the Reformation, but there is some original stained glass – the fine east window of the north transept was restored in 1970 – a large 15th-century tomb in the south transept and the Cheney monument in the nave.

The church was restored by C.E. Ponting between 1887 and 1891, who put in the nave altar. The high altar with its carved reredos was designed by Randoll Blacking and introduced in 1936. Various brass consecration crosses have also been restored.

BELOW: *The early Perpendicular church took only ten years to build in the mid-14th century.*

ST MARY, POTTERNE

WILTSHIRE

his unusual 13th-century cruciform church sits on the edge of a steep hillside filled with sunken lanes and looks westwards across the lower landscape of north-west Wiltshire. The manor of Potterne was given to the Bishop of Sherborne in the Anglo-Saxon period. It then passed to the Bishop of Salisbury. Bishop Osmund, who was later canonised, gave the church to the canons of his new cathedral at Old Sarum in 1091, where it became a rich prebend. Between 1225 and 1245 it was the prebend of Master Elias of Dereham, who was the canon in charge of building Salisbury Cathedral.

The present church must have been built by Elias himself in the 1230s as one can see instantly that it resembles a miniature Salisbury Cathedral, with its crossing tower, large transepts, pairs

and triplets of lancet windows and shafts of Purbeck marble. The more elaborate east window is extremely close in style to the much larger high east window at Salisbury Cathedral, with a stepped group of five lancets. All of this is no coincidence, and it seems very likely that Elias of Dereham actually designed Salisbury Cathedral, in addition to his own little church. He is also known to have designed buildings for Henry III and, most famously, he was one of two designers of the shrine of St Thomas Becket in Canterbury Cathedral in 1220.

The tower at Potterne was given elaborate battlements with Perpendicular tracery added to its windows in the 15th century; however, the original 13th-century windows – pairs of lancets with a quatrefoil in a circle above – can still be very clearly seen. This style is known as plate tracery, the earliest form of tracery used in England, and once again similar windows can be seen in the west front of Salisbury Cathedral. It

is surely no exaggeration to describe Elias as the Christopher Wren of the early 13th century.

In 1255, ten years after the death of Elias of Dereham, the prebend of Potterne was given back to the Bishop of Salisbury, and it remains in his possession some 750 years later. No further building work was done on the church in the later Middle Ages, apart from the addition of porches and Perpendicular work on the tower. Inside the church is a remarkable Anglo-Saxon tub-font, with a Latin inscription round the rim. It was presumably kept from the earlier church that stood here.

OPPOSITE, RIGHT: *The view east to the crossing and chancel, with the fine east window flanked by shafts of Purbeck marble.*

BELOW: *From the south-west, the church's 15th-century additions to the tower, tracery and parapets are clearly visible.*

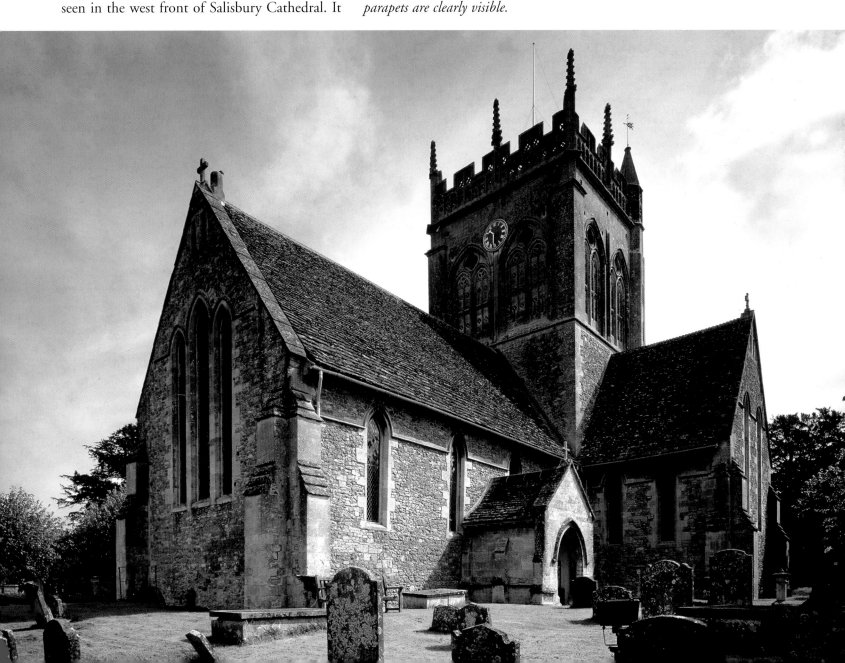

ST MARY REDCLIFFE, BRISTOL

AVON

ABOVE: *This central vaulting boss in the north nave aisle represents a labyrinth.*

BELOW: *The bold double-aisled south transept dominates the church's south façade.*

Bristol was one of the greatest cities of late medieval England, and until the dreadful destruction of the Second World War, it was full of fine parish churches. The finest of them all – St Mary Redcliffe – narrowly missed destruction in 1941, and remains one of the most magnificent parish churches in England. When St Mary's was first built it was constructed outside the southern city wall, beside the port.

The church is first documented in the early 12th century, when it was given to Salisbury Cathedral by Henry I (1100–1135), along with the neighbouring royal manor of Bedminster. This became a very rich prebend in the cathedral, and it is surely no coincidence that St Mary Redcliffe has a splendid, 292-foot (89-metre) tall stone tower and spire which are of the same date and style as the spire at Salisbury itself. However, the spire here was struck by lightning in 1446, and the top two thirds fell on the church – it was rebuilt only in 1872.

Contemporary with the upper part of the tower and spire is the wonderful hexagonal outer north porch. This was added at the beginning of the 14th century, and its sumptuous ornate Decorated architecture is unsurpassed almost anywhere. There are three doorways on the three northern sides, which open into an exceptionally beautiful vaulted space (see page 13).

The church itself is one of the largest parish churches in England with aisled nave, chancel and transepts. There is an ambulatory behind the high altar, with a projecting Lady chapel beyond it. The whole building is 240 feet (73 metres) long inside. There are also stone vaults throughout, clerestories and, as already mentioned, a very large tower and spire. St Mary Redcliffe is, in everything but name, a cathedral.

The rebuilding of the church started in the later 14th century and

BELOW: *The superb 14th-century corbels of Dundry stone were removed from the north porch and are now displayed in the north nave aisle.*

RIGHT: *The spectacular vaulted nave and chancel, with the separate Lady chapel in the distance.*

BELOW RIGHT: *Effigies of William Canynge the Younger and his wife, Joanna, on his tomb.*

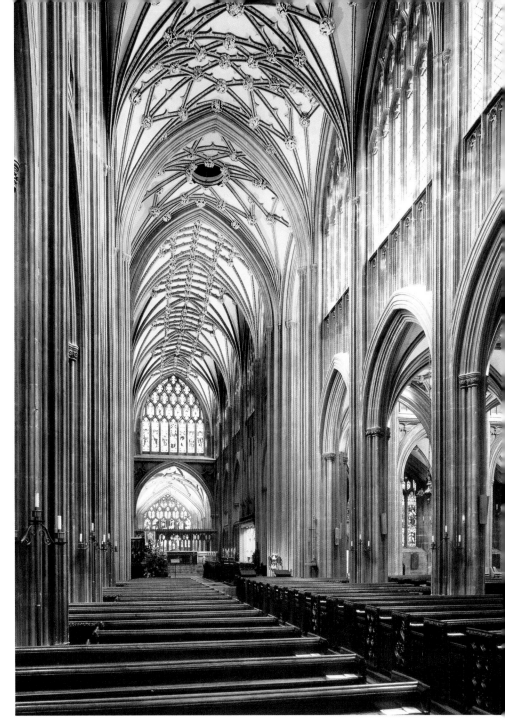

continued on into the 15th century, when Bristol, and particularly its port, was at the peak of its prosperity. Many rich merchants no doubt contributed to the work, but it was the Canynge family who are most heavily associated with the church, in particular William Canynge the Younger, who was five times mayor of Bristol and twice its Member of Parliament. He financed the completion of the church after the fall of the spire, and paid for most of the very costly high vaults and the high panelled work of the clerestories. At the end of his life, after the death of his wife in 1467, Canynge took holy orders, and his two alabaster effigies in the church represent him both with his wife and as a priest. He died in 1474.

THE WESTERN COUNTIES

These are all counties where good building stone can be found, and some of the churches contain superbly carved sculpture and masonry. It is also a very rich sheep area containing some of the greatest 'wool' churches, such as Cirencester, Burford and Fairford, and some key town churches, including Shrewsbury, Oxford, Ledbury, and Ludlow. The diversity is great. Acton Burnell is a small 'private' church for a very influential 13th-century bishop, whereas Warwick contains the grandest chantry chapel in England; wonderful wall paintings survive at Kempley, and Ewelme is part of a splendid complex of buildings with its cloistered almshouse and school.

OPPOSITE: *This finely carved reredos made by E.B. Hoare in the early 20th century sits behind the Lady chapel altar in St John the Baptist's, Burford.*

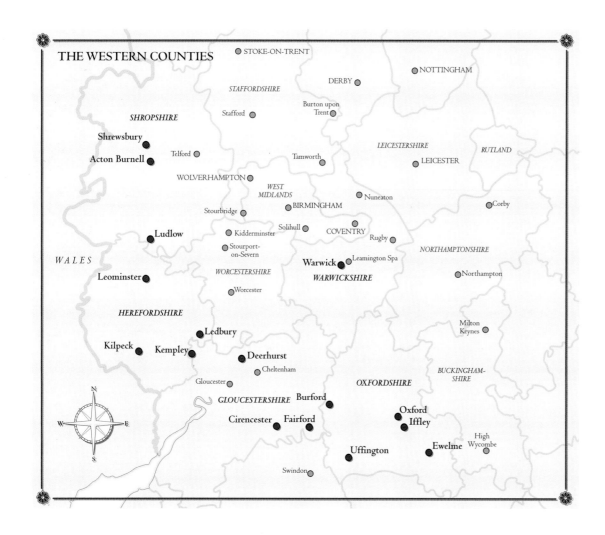

THE WESTERN COUNTIES

STOKE-ON-TRENT

NOTTINGHAM

DERBY

STAFFORDSHIRE

Burton upon Trent

SHROPSHIRE

Stafford

Shrewsbury

Telford

Tamworth

LEICESTERSHIRE

RUTLAND

Acton Burnell

LEICESTER

WOLVERHAMPTON

WEST MIDLANDS

Nuneaton

Corby

Stourbridge

BIRMINGHAM

Ludlow

Kidderminster

Solihull

COVENTRY

Rugby

NORTHAMPTONSHIRE

WALES

Stourport-on-Severn

WORCESTERSHIRE

Warwick

Leamington Spa

WARWICKSHIRE

Northampton

Leominster

Worcester

HEREFORDSHIRE

Milton Keynes

Ledbury

Kilpeck

Kempley

Deerhurst

BUCKINGHAM-SHIRE

Cheltenham

Gloucester

OXFORDSHIRE

Burford

GLOUCESTERSHIRE

Oxford

Cirencester

Fairford

Iffley

Uffington

Ewelme

High Wycombe

Swindon

ST MARY, EWELME

OXFORDSHIRE

About 12 miles (19km) south-east of Oxford, on the north-western edge of the Chilterns, is the little village of Ewelme, which takes its name from the spring (*æwelme*) in the village centre. Nearby is a wonderful complex of largely 15th-century buildings, with a still functioning brick almshouse that was built round a cloister at its centre; a schoolhouse that is still in use to the south-west; and the church to the north-east. The church is set in its own graveyard, but it is connected with the almshouse by a delightful covered passage that runs downhill to the almshouse cloister from under the west tower. The only thing that has been destroyed is the magnificent brick palace of the Earl and Countess of Suffolk, which lay not far away to the west.

William de la Pole (1396–1450) and his wife, Alice, who was the granddaughter of the poet, Geoffrey Chaucer (1344–1400), founded the almshouse and the church's chantry in 1437. De la Pole became the Duke of Suffolk in 1448; he was a key political figure in the early part of the reign of Henry VI (1422–61, 1470–71), and was murdered while crossing the English Channel in 1450.

The magnificent chantry chapel of St John the Baptist, which is on the south-eastern side of the church, is the most interesting part of the building. The splendid tomb of Alice de la Pole lies within the chapel. It has an elaborately decorated tomb-chest that is surmounted by an effigy of Alice wearing a ducal coronet and the Order of the Garter twisted round her left arm. At the base of the tomb, and visible through traceried openings, is a very realistic alabaster cadaver effigy of Alice contemplating the painted figures of the Annunciation, with St Mary Magdalene and St John the Baptist, on the ceiling. This tomb is set within an elaborately decorated opening between the chancel and the chapel. To the west of it is the tomb of Thomas and Maud Chaucer (Alice's parents), on top of which they are represented by a fine pair of brasses. This tomb was relocated here in about 1438, in the early stages of the de la Poles' rebuilding of the church.

Earlier, Sir Thomas Chaucer, who died in 1435, rebuilt the south aisle of the church using fine stone masonry. The rebuilding of the rest of the church used rubble masonry, except for the crenellated parapets which are of brick. This 'new' material was just coming into use in the mid-15th century, and it is in the beautiful almshouse and school down the hill that visitors can view this early red brick at its best.

BELOW: *Ninian Comper's altar and painted reredos in the chapel of St John the Baptist. The stencilled lettering on the east wall is a Victorian copy of the medieval.*

ST MARY, IFFLEY

OXFORDSHIRE

ABOVE: *This 12th-century carved boss, or keystone, sits at the apex of the Romanesque rib-vault in the sanctuary.*

BELOW: *John Piper's Nativity window, which brightens the north side of the baptistry, was gifted to the church in 1995 by Myfanwy Piper in memory of her husband.*

I ffley has now been engulfed by Oxford; however, the village's parish church, 2 miles (3.2km) south of the city centre, is still relatively isolated. The church was first built in the middle of the 12th century and was initially attached to the manor house, now Court Place, to the south. The owners of the manor at this time were the St Remy family, who spent much money on the construction of a highly decorated new church with the fairly common plan of nave, eastern tower and small square sanctuary.

Much of this original church survives, although the central window and upper arches in the west front were reconstructed in the 19th century. Of exceptional interest is the large amount of late Romanesque carved detail that is used in the church. Much of this is chevron or zig-zag decoration and 'beak-head', as it is known, but there are also some fine carved figures outside the south doorway and a beautiful hood-mould with lion heads linking 16 medallions above the principal west doorway. It was quite common for a Norman nave to have three doorways,

which were particularly used for processions.

Inside the church are two more finely decorated arches, which linked the nave, tower and sanctuary. One extremely rare feature is the use of monolithic black Tournai marble shafts in the church on either side of the two west faces of the arches. Tournai marble, which comes from the Franco–Belgian border, was usually only used as a luxury building material in the extreme south-east of England during the mid-12th century. There is another Tournai shaft in the upper part of the west front, and the font bowl is also of Tournai marble. Another unusual feature is the fine 12th-century stone vault in the sanctuary.

The tower is also 12th-century, although the upper part was almost completely rebuilt

between 1974 and 1983. The nave roof was lowered and given a new crenellated south parapet in 1612, but the original pitch of the roof was restored in the 19th century, along with the west gable.

Early in the 13th century, the east wall of the sanctuary was removed and an enlarged chancel was built. This, too, had a quadripartite stone vault and buttresses were later added round the chancel to support it. The final change was to put in new three-light Perpendicular windows at the east end of the nave and beneath the tower. This was done in the late 15th century, when a rood screen, which has since been removed, was also installed. The 19th-century restorations of the church were sensitively done.

ABOVE: *From the south-west the fine 12th-century south and west doorways can be seen. The west doorway is covered in chevron decoration.*

OPPOSITE: *The view east to the 13th-century chancel, with the 12th-century tower arches and their black marble shafts in front.*

ST MARY, OXFORD

OXFORDSHIRE

ABOVE: *The Radcliffe Camera can be seen through the north aisle window.*

BELOW: *The clerestoried nave dates from the late 15th century. The famous pulpit is on the right.*

Oxford University's parish church sits on the north side of the High Street, at the very centre of the city's many famous colleges. Immediately to the north are the Radcliffe Camera, the Old Bodleian Library and the Schools' Quadrangle. There may have been an Anglo-Saxon church on the site, which would have been rebuilt in the early Norman period before the university came into existence. The earliest visible remains, however, are those of the large buttressed north tower, which was constructed at the end of the 13th century. On top of this is the fine stone spire, which was put up in the early 14th century. It is worth noting that the two bishops who built the incomparable tower and spire of Salisbury Cathedral were successive chancellors of Oxford in the late 13th century.

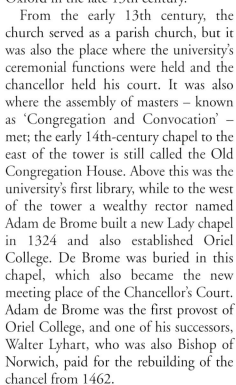

From the early 13th century, the church served as a parish church, but it was also the place where the university's ceremonial functions were held and the chancellor held his court. It was also where the assembly of masters – known as 'Congregation and Convocation' – met; the early 14th-century chapel to the east of the tower is still called the Old Congregation House. Above this was the university's first library, while to the west of the tower a wealthy rector named Adam de Brome built a new Lady chapel in 1324 and also established Oriel College. De Brome was buried in this chapel, which also became the new meeting place of the Chancellor's Court. Adam de Brome was the first provost of Oriel College, and one of his successors, Walter Lyhart, who was also Bishop of Norwich, paid for the rebuilding of the chancel from 1462.

From 1487, the university raised funds to rebuild the rest of the church, work that was completed by 1510. The well-lit aisled nave and chancel, which were constructed in the late Perpendicular style, were the result, and can be viewed from the High Street. There is an anomaly in the church's construction, however – the Baroque south porch, which was rebuilt to the design of Nicholas Stone in 1637.

RIGHT: *The spectacular façade of the church, as seen from the High Street. The Baroque porch can just be glimpsed behind the tree.*

BELOW: *At the base of the spire are niches covered in ballflower decoration, with 19th-century statues of St John the Evangelist (left) and of Walter de Merton, Bishop of Rochester and founder of Merton College, Oxford (right).*

Throughout its history the church has been the setting for famous sermons, trials and disputes. It was here that Archbishop Cranmer (1489–1556) was tried and it is also where he withdrew his recantation. He was burnt at the stake as a heretic in 1556 in nearby Broad Street. The church's most famous vicar, however, was John Henry Newman (1801–90), who came to the post in 1828. During Newman's tenure at the church, John Keble (1792–1866) preached his famous 'Assize' sermon in 1833, which began the High-Church Oxford Movement. Newman later resigned his post and was received into the Roman Catholic church in 1845, going on to reach the position of cardinal.

ST MARY, UFFINGTON

OXFORDSHIRE

This church, which is almost entirely 13th-century, lies in the vale that takes its name from the famous prehistoric White Horse that is cut in the downs above it. This area is now called South Oxfordshire, but for centuries it was part of Berkshire and within the diocese of Salisbury. The most important institution in this area in the Middle Ages was Abingdon Abbey, which was situated to the north-east of Uffington. The church of St Mary was one of a number that belonged to the abbey in this area.

The present church must have been built by Abingdon Abbey, although the building's architecture has much in common with its real mother church –

Salisbury Cathedral. Both buildings were dedicated to the Virgin Mary, and were constructed at exactly the same time, using double or triple lancets. One feature points directly to Salisbury Cathedral for its inspiration – the circular fixings for the brass consecration crosses. When a new church was started, the ritual required that three crosses should be put on each of the cardinal faces, so that the bishop could dedicate them. In almost every case the crosses were painted on the walls, but at Salisbury Cathedral elaborate circular fittings were made for brass crosses in the outer walls. At Uffington, simpler versions of these survive, although without the brasses. In the east and west walls, three circular discs can be seen, with the fixing holes inside them for the crosses. On the sides of the church, the crosses were spread out, and can be seen on the nave, transept and chancel. On the north side of the chancel, the cross must have been on the sacristy, which has since been demolished.

The architecture of this church, although modest compared to Salisbury Cathedral, is still of exceptional quality and interest. The inside of the chancel, with its internally shafted continuous rows of windows, was meant to have a stone vault over its eastern sanctuary. The transepts have projecting altar-spaces in their east sides – two on the north and one on the south – and these are covered with highly unusual triangular gables and triangular-shaped lancet window-heads. It has been questioned whether these really are 13th-century at all. However, the masonry used is the same as for the other 13th-century work and one double aumbry (cupboard) in Salisbury Cathedral also has triangular heads. The pair of lancets on either side of the eastern end of the nave had their tops cut off in the 17th century. They may also have had triangular heads.

On the south side, each of the doorways has a protective area on the exterior, which are also original features. For the south transept and chancel these are little more than elaborate canopies, but the nave has a fine vaulted porch with a 'parvise chamber' over it. There is also a moulded gable top, with pinnacles on either side and trefoil-headed statue niches. Once again, this is a miniature version of the great north porch at Salisbury.

Over the crossing is an octagonal tower, the top stage of which was built in 1746, after an earlier spire was destroyed in a gale in 1740.

BELOW: *The 13th-century church has an 18th-century top to its octagonal tower. On the chancel and south transept walls are consecration cross fittings.*

ST JOHN THE BAPTIST, BURFORD

OXFORDSHIRE

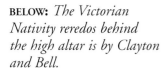

Burford is a beautiful medieval cloth town on the western boundary of Oxfordshire beside the River Windrush. It grew up on the main road between Oxford and the Cotswolds (now the A40) in the middle of an important group of quarries that produced the very fine Taynton stone, which, not surprisingly, was used in the construction of this church.

The church is a remarkable, irregular structure with features dating from each century between the 12th and the 16th. The rectory of Burford and the neighbouring chapelry of Fulbrook were given to Keynsham Abbey near Bristol by William, Earl of Gloucester in about 1170. This is the approximate date of the earliest parts of the church, including the long nave and central tower with, to the east of it, a small sanctuary – a similar plan to the church at Iffley (see pages 66–7). Much of the fine crossing tower and the arches between the nave, the tower and the sanctuary beneath it still exist. The 12th-century west doorway and lower part of the nave's west wall also survive, and the beautiful decorative hinges on the outside of the west doors are still the original 12th-century ironwork.

In the 13th century, a larger chancel was built with side chapels, and a north and south transept to the west. A small south aisle was also added to the nave. In the later 14th century, a raised chantry chapel, dedicated to St Thomas Becket, was added to the west of the south transept. At the eastern end of the nave, the memorial brass of John Spycer, who died in 1437, tells us that he paid for the 'rode soler' (rood loft) and a 'gabulwyndow' in the church. The rood

loft, which is above the grave, has sadly gone, but the gable window is probably the one that can still be seen on the south side of the chapel of St Thomas.

The main rebuilding and enlargement of the church got under way in the 15th century, and this may have started with the upper stage of the tower and the slender stone spire. Unfortunately, the 12th-century lower stage started to crack, and the north and south arches below the tower had to be partially filled in with extra buttresses. The north transept and the north-east chapels were also remodelled, but the principal work was the complete reconstruction of the nave and aisles with new arcades and large windows, including the clerestories and, as a late addition, a beautiful three-storey, fan-vaulted south porch. To the south-west of the church was a separate 13th-century guild Lady chapel in the church-yard. At the end of the 15th century this was rebuilt on the south and joined to the south-west end of the nave as a new chapel of St Mary and St Anne (its 20th-century reredos can be seen on page 63).

All the altars and chantries were, of course, removed during the Reformation, but family pews remained in several of them. The north-east chapel contains the very large and fine monument to Sir Lawrence Tanfield and his wife. He was the lord of the surrounding manor and Lord Chief Baron of the Court of Exchequer under James I. When Tanfield died in 1625, his wife had the monument erected in 'the aisle adjoining the communion chancel on the north' without asking the churchwardens' permission!

OPPOSITE: *The memorial to Robert Silvester (died 1601) in the south-west chapel contains the phrase 'Christ is to me Life, deathe is to me advantage'.*

RIGHT: *The 12th-century crossing tower has an upper stage and spire that date from the 15th century.*

ST MARY, FAIRFORD

GLOUCESTERSHIRE

F airford lies on the River Coln, a few miles above its junction with the Thames, where the counties of Wiltshire, Oxfordshire and Gloucestershire meet. It was one of several rich cloth towns in the lower Cotswolds. The church of St Mary was given to Tewkesbury Abbey at the end of the 11th century, but the earliest visible remains are fragments of the eastern ends of the 13th-century arcades, which were preserved by the tower piers.

Apart from the tower piers themselves, the whole of the church was rebuilt at the end of the 15th century and the beginning of the 16th century. Most of the money for the building work came from a rich clothier named John Tame and his son Edmund. Tame was already a rich man in 1479, when he leased the royal manor of Fairford with his father-in-law, John Twyniho. By the 1490s, Tame had determined to pay for the rebuilding of the whole church. When he died in 1500, much of the work must have been completed. He was buried beneath a fine Purbeck marble tomb-chest that was decorated with a brass of himself and his wife, Alice. The tomb lies between the chancel and the Lady chapel to the north of the church.

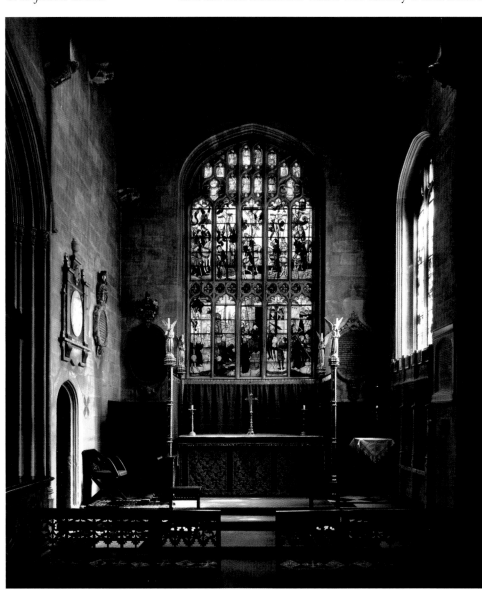

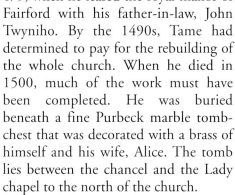

Tame's son Edmund completed the rebuilding work, and was responsible for the installation of the furnishings and stained glass. Amazingly, the original stained glass still survives in all the church's windows, although some of it has been badly damaged, particularly the west windows, which suffered during the great storm of 1703. This building is the only church in England to contain a complete set of its pre-Reformation glass, and the twenty-eight windows display a single comprehensive scheme.

In the Lady chapel, the stained glass depicts the life of the Virgin and the birth of Christ; the east window depicts the crucifixion of Jesus; while Pentecost is celebrated in the window of the Corpus Christi chapel. In the nave aisles and clerestory, by contrast, images of saints, martyrs, apostles, prophets and evangelists can be seen. The great

west window shows an image of Christ in Majesty with a Doom scene beneath it.

Since 1988, many of the windows have been cleaned, repaired, reinstalled and protected, and the visitor can now better appreciate this unique collection of high-quality early 16th-century glass. The original screens that divide the eastern (chancel) part of the church also survive, as do the parclose screens to the north and south chapels.

The young Henry VIII knighted Edmund Tame in 1516, and four years later the king visited Fairford for a week, almost certainly to see the completed church. By this time, Sir Edmund was also a wealthy member of the royal household and steward for life of the lordship of Fairford. His pristine new church must have looked spectacular. The last part of the building to be completed was probably the upper part of the tower, with decorated shields and strange statues, which were, no doubt, brightly painted.

ST JOHN THE BAPTIST, CIRENCESTER

GLOUCESTERSHIRE

Cirencester's church of St John the Baptist is the largest and most splendid parish church in the Cotswolds, an area that is replete with many fine late medieval churches. The reason for Cirencester's dominance is that, compared to other towns in the region, it has a long and complex history, which started with the construction of Britain's second-largest Roman city – Corinium. By the late Anglo-Saxon period, a very large church existed here, situated to the north-east of the present church.

In the early 12th century, the Saxon church was rebuilt as a large monastic church for an Augustinian Abbey founded by Henry I. At the same time, a large new cruciform parish church was built on the south-west corner of the abbey precinct, beside the new market-place. Fragments of the shell of this church survive in the present building, and the north and south transepts at the eastern end of the nave were not replaced until the 15th century. By the late 13th century, the chancel had been extended and small chapels were added on either side. A large, almost detached, Lady chapel was also built on the north-eastern side of the building. By the 14th century, the town was becoming very wealthy on the profits of the wool trade.

During the battle for the crown between Richard II (1377–99) and Henry of Bolingbroke (1366–1416, later Henry IV), two of Richard II's half brothers, John and Thomas, were seized by the townspeople and executed in Cirencester's market-place. As a result of the town's loyalty, the town prospered under Henry IV, and the abbey and the wool merchants, who had previously resented one another, worked together to enlarge the parish church, which was overlooked from the north-east by the abbey's own church. The reconstruction began with the west tower, but when it was half built, its foundations started to settle over the Roman walls and ditches beneath, so two huge flying buttresses had to be constructed at the western ends of the aisles.

In the 1430s, a beautiful new chapel was built for the weavers' Guild of the Holy Trinity on the north side of the church; it contains some very fine brasses, which were gathered together in 1867, at the eastern end of the building. A little later the Lady chapel was rebuilt on the eastern side of the church, as was the chapel of St Catherine and St Nicholas, which

ABOVE: *Angels adorn the heads of the nave pillars.*

BELOW: *The huge three-storeyed south porch sits on Cirencester's market-place, with the west tower just behind.*

ABOVE: *The spectacular stone pulpit dates from the 15th century and sits on the north-east side of the nave.*

LEFT: *Slender columns and large clerestory windows dominate the nave.*

was constructed as a chantry for John Chedworth, the Bishop of Lincoln. In 1508, this chapel was heightened and extended, and given a beautiful fan-vault by Abbot Hakebourne.

Between about 1516 and 1525 an amazing reconstruction of the entire nave was undertaken. The result was a space with tall, slender piers and high clerestory windows – so high that there are also clerestory windows in the outer wall above the Trinity chapel. Just before this work was done, the abbot had built the largest and most splendid south porch of any church in England. A great north–south passage, covered with a fan-vault and with doors into the churchyard, was constructed on either side of the church for processions. Above this were two storeys of very grand rooms, intended for the abbey's secular meetings. Each chamber had a row of oriel windows looking out onto the market-place.

After the Dissolution of the abbey between 1539 and 1540, this building became the town hall, although it reverted to the vicar and churchwardens in 1671. After the Reformation, the church went into decline, although George Gilbert Scott undertook a major restoration between 1865 and 1867.

ST MARY, DEERHURST

GLOUCESTERSHIRE

St Mary's Church at Deerhurst, which sits on the banks of the River Severn, is only 2 miles (3.2km) south-west of the more famous Tewkesbury Abbey. In the 9th century, Deerhurst was the site of one of the most important monasteries in the area, and, unlike similar establishments, substantial elements from the late Anglo-Saxon building survive in the present church. In the mid-11th century, the church came under the control of the family of Earl Odda, who built his own private chapel nearby. This chapel, which was dedicated in 1056, still survives and is in the care of English Heritage.

Just before the Norman Conquest in 1066, Deerhurst was divided into two halves by Edward the Confessor – one part was given to Westminster Abbey, while the other was given to the king's doctor, Baldwin, who was a monk of the Abbey of St Denis, near Paris. St Denis and Westminster became the most famous royal abbeys in France and England, and after the Conquest a monastic cell of St Denis was created at Deerhurst. Traces of the cloister can still be seen on the exterior to the south of the church, and to the east some of the 14th-century monastic buildings survive in Priory House.

The present parish church consists of a west tower, which dates almost entirely from the late Anglo-Saxon period; a nave with side chapels and aisles that were taken west to flank the tower; a chancel that is at one with the nave; and a ruined apse to the east, which has been archaeologically excavated and was once the chancel. The late Anglo-Saxon chancel arch is now blocked, but it can be seen behind the altar.

The architectural development of the Anglo-Saxon church was clearly very complicated, and archaeologists are still trying to work out its complete history. However, many interesting features are evident and much sculptural decoration can be seen, including several 'primitive' triangular-headed openings, various carved animal heads and a sculpture of the Virgin and Child. Pride of place must go to the remarkable font, which

BELOW: *The remains of the cloister north wall are still visible below the aisle windows when viewed from the south-west.*

probably dates from the 9th century and is covered in spiral decorations. Also worthy of note is the Byzantine-like angel, which is mounted high on the southern corner of the church's exterior.

Other building work dates from the later medieval period, including the 13th-century arcades and some excellent early 14th-century stained glass. Stained glass dating from the 15th century depicts the figure of St Alphege (954–1012). He was a remarkable man who was a monk at Deerhurst in the mid-10th century, before becoming Bishop of Winchester in 984 and Archbishop of Canterbury in 1006, at a time when the Viking hordes were overrunning England. The Vikings captured him after the siege of Canterbury in 1011, and when he refused to be ransomed he was pelted to death with ox bones at Greenwich.

ST MARY, KEMPLEY

GLOUCESTERSHIRE

U nusually, this is no longer the parish church, because a brand-new one was built in 1903 at the more populous heart of the parish. The original church, which was close to the old manor house, Kempley Court, is farther north. It is officially redundant, but is well cared for by English Heritage. The church, which was built in the mid-12th century, survives intact and still contains three great rarities: its original roof, although it was modified in 1670 when a ceiling was put in; its original frescoes on the wall; and the barrel-vault of the chancel. Other original features include the sculpture on the chancel arch; the west and south doorways; three original wooden doors, which have their original hinges, at the western and southern ends; and the south chancel doorway. For good measure, the church also contains a medieval wooden chest.

ABOVE: *The 12th-century west door to the nave has been there since the church was first built.*

BELOW: *The simple nave, which leads into the barrel-vaulted chancel, has a series of 14th-century wall paintings.*

ABOVE: *The Norman church has a 13th-century west tower.*

RIGHT: *Twelfth-century frescoes of apostles still adorn the north wall of the chancel.*

has been protected from the weather by a 14th-century wooden porch, and just visible at the back of this is a 'Tree of Life' carving on the tympanum over the Norman doorway. There are similar sculptures elsewhere in the area, including one at nearby Dymock, which implies that there must have been a local school of masons in the area during the 12th century.

The wall paintings in the chancel were true frescoes (painted on wet plaster), but unfortunately, soon after they were rediscovered in 1872 they were treated with shellac, a heavy varnish that darkens with age. This was removed between 1955 and 1958, and the chancel is now a wonderful space that gives some impression of what many mid-12th-century sanctuaries looked like. In the nave, the wall paintings are less well preserved and mainly of the 14th century. They are done as tempera, a pigment in soluble glue. Visitors can still, therefore, progress from the more fragmentary scenes in the nave, which include a Doom painting over the chancel arch, to the wonderfully complete scenes in the chancel, where the focus is Christ seated on a rainbow in the act of Benediction. All around him are figures and symbols that provide a remarkable insight into the 12th-century Christian mind.

In the 12th century, many new churches were built in England with simple rectangular naves and chancels, but in almost every case the church was enlarged or modified in the later Middle Ages. At Kempley, the only major addition was the sturdy 13th-century west tower, which has a squat pyramidal roof and no external doorway. The Norman south doorway

ST MICHAEL, LEDBURY

HEREFORDSHIRE

From Anglo-Saxon times Ledbury was an important settlement in south-eastern Herefordshire; however, it was only in the 12th century that it became a major town, under the patronage of the bishops of Hereford. A large triangular market-place was created with plots for houses placed all around it. Just up the hillside to the east, the Anglo-Saxon church was demolished and a large aisled building, which is still the core of the present structure, was erected. It had a long, six-bay nave with large, round pillars and lean-to aisles on either side. Only the round bases of the north aisle can still be seen, but the very fine western doorway and much of the central part of the west front of the church survives.

East of the large nave, between the beautiful compound piers of the chancel arch, which dates from the late 12th century, steps lead up to an equally large chancel. This already had lean-to chapels on either side, which were entered through the two bays of round arches that still exist. Above the arches are three round windows on either side, which looked out over the original lean-to roofs. Farther east, up another flight of steps, is the sanctuary, which originally had two round-headed windows on either side, although these were replaced by large Perpendicular windows in the 14th century. Another early rarity is the survival of the double round-headed aumbries (cupboards) on either side of the church, as well as one in the north aisle chapel.

In the early 13th century, the north arcade may have become unstable and been rebuilt. At about the same time, and perhaps because of the unstable conditions, a free-standing stone bell-tower was built to the north. A timber and lead covered spire originally crowned this tower, but between 1727 and 1734 the present upper stage was built and topped with a magnificent stone spire that stretches up over 200 feet (60 metres).

Later in the 13th century, the whole of the north aisle was rebuilt with a new enlarged chapel at the eastern end, which is now a vestry. This aisle has beautiful three-light windows in the style of the magnificent north transept of nearby Hereford Cathedral, built by Bishop Aquablanca. Even more splendid is the south aisle, which was rebuilt in about 1300; with its

ABOVE: *Detail of a carved head on the 17th-century font.*

BELOW: *The sanctuary has an 1824 copy of Leonardo da Vinci's* The Last Supper *over the high altar.*

fine plinth and buttresses, this looks particularly remarkable from the south side of the church-yard. The south nave arcade was rebuilt at the same time, followed some time later by the north arcade.

The high point, however, is the so-called 'Chapter House', which was added to the north aisle in about 1320. This has magnificent traceried windows that are all covered in ball-flower decoration, with double sunk-chamfers on all the window jambs. This room, the original function of which is unknown, also contains an outstanding canopied effigy of a priest praying, which dates from the late 13th century and was originally a horizontal tomb-cover. The church also contains many fine later monuments; one of the finest – a lady on a tomb-chest dating from the late 14th century – is tucked away in the vestry at the eastern end of the north aisle. It is covered in shields, but unfortunately the canopy is gone.

ABOVE: *Angels appear in the window of the Nativity, which was designed by Sir Edward Burne-Jones and made in the William Morris workshop.*

LEFT: *The magnificent early 18th-century stone spire sits atop the freestanding bell-tower.*

ST MARY AND ST DAVID, KILPECK

HEREFORDSHIRE

This famous 12th-century parish church has been described as 'one of the most perfect Norman village churches in England'. This is because the church still has its original nave, chancel and apsidal sanctuary, which were all probably built as one in the 1130s. The most magnificent feature of all is the wonderful Romanesque carving on the south and west doors, the chancel arch and the corbels all round the outside of the church.

The main reason that the entire Norman church was preserved was because it was built at the centre of a new 12th-century castle borough that did not develop in the later Middle Ages. Immediately to the west of the church are the extensive earthworks for a motte and bailey castle and the remains of a polygonal shell keep, while in the fields on either side of the road to the north-east of the church (the former High Street) are the humps and bumps of the plots of abandoned houses, which are surrounded by the outer bank and ditch for the town defences. The present village of Kilpeck is largely outside the former town to the south.

ABOVE: *Detail of the remarkable corbel table at the corner of the nave.*

BELOW: *The apsidal sanctuary, chancel and nave, viewed from the south-east, all date from the 12th century and are in excellent condition.*

BELOW AND OPPOSITE:
The carving found all over the church at Kilpeck is outstanding. Scandinavian-style figures carved on either side of the south door-way are particularly impressive, as is the Tree of Life in the tympanum above.

Hereford Cathedral, which lies some 7 miles (11km) to the north-east of Kilpeck, underwent a rebuild at the beginning of the 12th century, and in 1134 a new Benedictine priory was founded at Kilpeck as a cell of Gloucester Abbey. This has disappeared now, but masons probably came out from Hereford to build both the priory and the new parish church. The carving that they produced for the church has parallels with Romanesque carving from all over western Europe, including churches in Scandinavia, Santiago de Compostela in Spain and Ferrara in Italy. Scholars have demonstrated how a new 'Herefordshire School' of carving began to develop at this time. The sculpture at Kilpeck, which is fashioned in Old Red Sandstone, is exceptional. The chancel arch has figures on either side and the apse at the church's eastern end has an early rib-vault that is covered with zig-zag decoration.

The church was sensitively restored by L.N. Cottingham in 1848. At the same time, new stained-glass windows were designed by Augustus Pugin (1812–52) for the apse. Finally, visitors must not fail to walk all the way round the outside of the church to view the amazing corbel table, with its large collection of totally secular carvings – some of which are rather rude.

RIGHT: *Inside the apsidal sanctuary are original rib-vaults covered in zig-zag decoration.*

ST PETER AND ST PAUL, LEOMINSTER

HEREFORDSHIRE

eominster, as its name suggests, was the site of an important Anglo-Saxon monastery church in northern Herefordshire, which was dissolved in 1046. In 1123, Henry I gave the manor to his newly founded royal abbey, which was ultimately his burial place, at Reading. A daughter house, in the shape of a Benedictine priory, was established at Leominster, and a large monastic church was quickly erected. This building was a smaller version of Reading Abbey itself, and we know from excavations that the eastern end of the structure had a large semicircular ambulatory that was surrounded by apsidal chapels. Unfortunately, all of this was pulled down soon after the dissolution of the monastery in 1539, and all that is left today is a large portion of a great aisled nave, which appears to have contained the parish church within it from the beginning.

On the southern side of the nave, two stages of enlargement of the parochial nave took place in the 13th and 14th centuries. This indicates how quickly the population of the new urban centre at Leominster was growing during this period. The town was first established around its triangular market-place in the 12th century, and it grew rapidly until the Black Death struck in the mid-14th century. It is interesting to note that the priory church is detached from the dense urban centre even today. This is because it was set in a large monastic precinct near the River

Lugg on the north-east side of the town.

Nothing of the eastern, monastic arm of the building is visible today, but the central part of the Norman nave and its north aisle still survive as very fine examples of the architecture of that period. The form of the piers in the nave is somewhat unusual and at the eastern and western ends the massive piers are pierced only by small doorways. This led some scholars to suggest that some sort of vaulting with domes was originally planned. In the event, a more conventional upper wall was built.

At the western end of the nave a Norman tower was planned, but never erected. It was not until the 15th century that the present tower was constructed, although its parapets and pinnacles date from the 19th century. Below the tower is the wide, slightly pointed west doorway, which was completed in the later 12th century. It has some finely carved figured capitals on either side.

In the early 13th century, the Norman south aisle was demolished and replaced by a much larger aisle for the parish. It was also given a fine south porch. Another south aisle was added at the beginning of the 14th century, and the south porch was taken down and rebuilt. All of this new work was characterized by the use of ballflower decoration.

Unfortunately, the whole church was gutted by fire on 18 March 1699, but the parishioners chose to rebuild in the old shell, rather than pull down the remains and put up a new church. The 18th-century fittings, which included the pews and galleries and a new south arcade, were all removed in the 1860s when the church was restored by George Gilbert Scott. The rather bare church that exists today is his creation – rather oddly, the church still also contains the parish ducking stool.

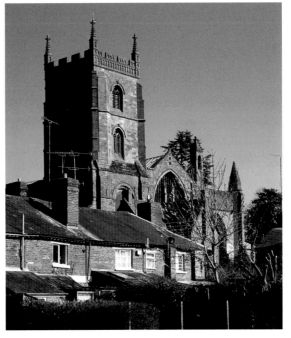

LEFT: *The dominant 15th-century tower from the north-west, with the great west window of the south aisle beyond.*

BELOW: *The fine 12th-century west doorway has beautifully carved figured capitals.*

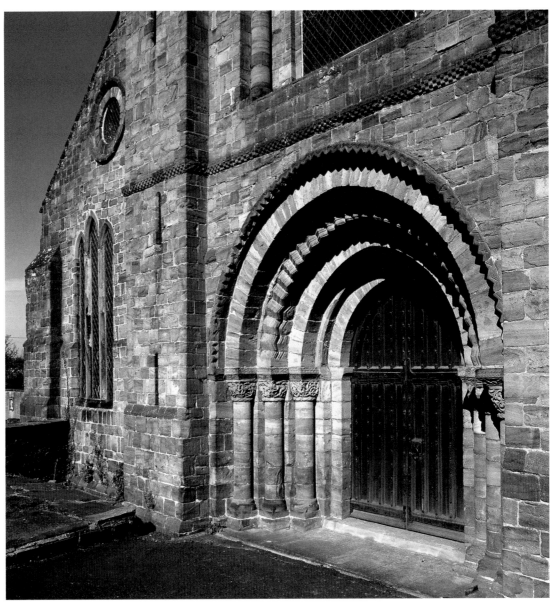

ST LAURENCE, LUDLOW

SHROPSHIRE

Ludlow is a magnificent hilltop town that is still dominated by its great castle, which was first built in the 11th century by Roger de Montgomery, Earl of Shrewsbury. To the east of the castle, a wide market-place was laid out in the early 12th century and a new town was planned around it. At the centre of the town a large church was built, which had probably acquired aisles by the end of the 12th century. The church is now approached from the south through narrow alleyways, because the eastern end of the market-place was filled in with 'middle rows' in the late Middle Ages. To see the external fabric of the building better, it is necessary to enter the churchyard on the north side – the city wall was to the north of this – and look back. The great 135-foot (40.5-metre) high crossing tower can, of course, be glimpsed from all over the town and beyond.

By the 13th century, Ludlow had become a prosperous wool town and a much bigger chancel would have been built; however, this was later replaced and only the fine moulded south

doorway survives from this period. In the early 14th century, with continuing prosperity, the townsmen started to rebuild the aisle walls, and we can see that this process started on the north-west side, where new windows with ballflower decoration were installed. A more ambitious building scheme was soon put in hand and large transept chapels were built on the north and south, followed by a remarkable new vaulted south porch. The porch is hexagonal in plan – only two other English churches have hexagonal porches, at Chipping Norton and St Mary Redcliffe in Bristol (see pages 60–61).

The Black Death and the problems of the later 14th century must have curtailed the building work for a time, but by the early 15th century the town was again very prosperous and the complete rebuilding of the chancel was put in hand. It was extended to the east but also greatly heightened – the roof is 52 feet (15.6 metres) above the ground – and the reconstruction in the Perpendicular style was a triumph. By 1447 the work was completed and the wood for the chancel stalls, which have many fine misericords under the seats, was acquired. At this point, work began to rebuild the nave arcades and heighten the walls.

This further work was probably interrupted by the Wars of the Roses, during which Ludlow was captured by the Lancastrians in 1459. The town's wealthy citizens were, however, determined to carry on, and a magnificent new crossing tower was constructed. The four large piers were placed towards the eastern end of the nave, and once the tall first stage was built, beautiful flying arches with double sunk-chamfers were erected to support the tower from the side walls of the transept. This necessitated the heightening of the transept walls and new upper windows were also installed. All this work, and the rebuilding of the new chantry chapels, was not finished until the late 15th century. The resulting building is, however, a masterpiece of the Perpendicular style. Much more money was spent on decorating and furnishing the church, and Ludlow is also lucky to have much magnificent late medieval stained glass.

BELOW LEFT: *On a monument to Theophilus Salwey, who died in 1760, a cherub looks at the symbols of death and resurrection.*

BELOW RIGHT: *The towering arches, in the north transept, and the great crossing arches dominate the view north-eastwards to the chancel.*

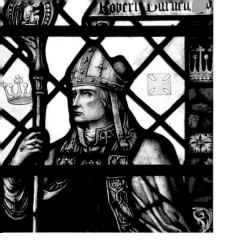

ST MARY, ACTON BURNELL

SHROPSHIRE

ABOVE: *The 19th-century glass on the north side of the chancel includes a portrait of Bishop Burnell.*

BELOW: *The 13th-century church, as seen from the north-east, with the 1889 tower in the centre.*

This fine later 13th-century church, in its beautiful setting, was built because a local man, Robert Burnell, was a great personal friend and private chaplain of Prince Edward, who in 1272 became King Edward I. Upon his accession to the throne, Edward made Burnell his Lord Chancellor and Bishop of Bath and Wells. The church here was probably built in the 1270s both for the parish and the neighbouring fortified manor house, Acton Burnell 'castle'. The ruined shell of the latter can still be seen over the churchyard wall in a picturesque landscape among parkland cedars. Construction of the castle probably began in the 1270s, although we know that it got an official licence for its crenellations in 1284, the year after Edward I came to Acton and held a parliament here. It must have been completed by 1292, which was when Robert died.

The church that survives is entirely the structure that was built in the 1270s, apart from a squat little tower over an organ chamber, which was added between 1887 and 1889. It has the usual nave and chancel, and, to the north and south, transept chapels. The architecture and masonry used in the church was of the most recent and up-to-date style in England, as befitted a great man of the time. Its closest parallel is at Wells, where the cathedral and cloister had recently been com-

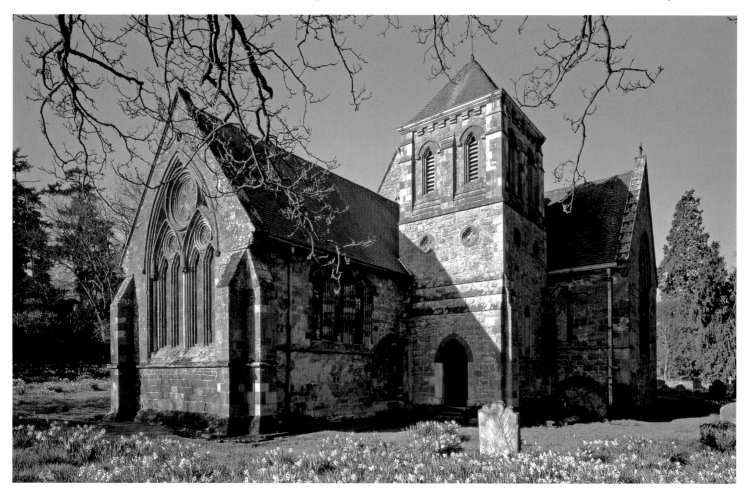

pleted, and where Robert Burnell was building himself a magnificent new great hall within his great moated palace. At Acton, the finest element is the chancel, which has a splendid four-light east window with trefoiled circles over it, above which is a large cinquefoiled circle. Along the sides of the chancel are groups of lancets with rounded trefoiled heads, and inside they all have monolithic marble nook shafts. The chancel and transept arches all have good concave mouldings and hoodmoulds, and there are large piscinas with stiff-leaf capitals over the shafts.

No additions were made to the church in the later Middle Ages, but the whole church was re-roofed in the Elizabethan period by the family of Sir Richard Lee, who died in 1591, and whose exceptionally fine alabaster tomb is situated in the north transept. Nearby is another excellent monument by Nicholas Stone, for Sir Richard's son, Sir Humphrey, who died in 1632. The most interesting tomb here is that of Sir Nicholas Burnell, who died in 1382, which has a fine brass on it. Remarkably, this transept still contains its original medieval tiled floor.

ABOVE: *Sir Richard Lee's elaborate alabaster tomb sits on the east side of the north transept, which has 13th-century mouldings and carved capitals.*

ST MARY, SHREWSBURY

SHROPSHIRE

S hrewsbury was the fortified gateway to mid-Wales. The town was established by the Normans on a large rocky hill in a great loop in the River Severn. The mouth of the loop was guarded by a royal castle and access to the town was by two fine bridges, the English one to the east and the Welsh one to the north-west. Just over the English bridge, a great Benedictine abbey was built, and this was the greatest church in Shrewsbury. After the Dissolution in the 16th century, only the nave was retained as a parish church. In the town itself were several parish churches, but the largest and finest, and probably the oldest with an Anglo-Saxon predecessor, was St Mary's. What survives today is still a very fine church with the third highest spire in England at 222 feet (67 metres). Sadly the church is no longer in use. It has recently been taken over by the Churches Conservation Trust, and the very fine collection of stained glass inside has been carefully restored.

The earliest parts of the present church, built mostly with the local Old Red Sandstone, are the nave, without its aisles, chancel and the lowest parts of the north and south transepts. The lower part of the west tower is obviously later 12th-century, as are the round-headed doorways at the ends of the transepts, which from the beginning had eastern chapels. At the start of the 13th century, aisles were added to the nave and the four beautiful bays of arcading on each side of this are the church's best architectural feature. They have slender piers and very fine stiff-leaf capitals.

The aisles originally had steeply sloping roofs, as can be seen in their end walls, but a very splendid gabled south porch was also built at this time which was given an upper storey in the early 14th century. The chancel was also remodelled in the early 13th century, and the tall pointed chancel arch, with a pair of two-light windows above, is particularly good. The upper end walls of the two transepts were also rebuilt with tall three-light windows.

In the early 14th century, a large new Trinity chapel, with windows with fine flowing tracery, was added on the south-east. It became the Drapers' Chapel in 1460.

In the late Middle Ages, the nave and aisles were rebuilt with many fine Perpendicular windows in the outer walls and clerestories. The top stage of the tower was also built at this time, with good two-light transomed Perpendicular bell-openings. The contemporary octagonal stone spire above is particularly fine, with three levels of dormers, and battlements and big pinnacles at its base.

Inside the church is a splendid display of stained glass; however, it is not the original medieval glass, but a collection including much continental glass, which was started by the early 19th-century vicar, W.G. Rowland. An exceptional window is the Jesse window in the chancel, which was probably made for the Franciscan church in Shrewsbury and then moved to the local church of St Chad's after the Reformation.

ABOVE: *The 12th-century west tower and early 13th-century south porch dominate the south-west side of the church.*

RIGHT: *A detail of the stained-glass east window, which depicts a tree growing out of Jesse's side, dates from c. 1340 and was previously in St Chad's, Shrewsbury.*

ST MARY, WARWICK

WARWICKSHIRE

arwick is now most famous for its most remarkable castle. The town, which is still relatively small, also has a magnificent great church at its centre. Unfortunately, a fire gutted the town of Warwick on 5 September 1694, and the whole of the western part of the church was burnt and had to be rebuilt. Sir Christopher Wren (1632–1723) submitted a sketch for the new church in 1696, but a local mason named Sir William Wilson, who had local connections, got the job. He rebuilt the nave, high aisles and transepts, but when he started to build a new west tower within the western end of the nave cracks started to appear. This meant that a separate tower had to be constructed outside the nave. This tower is 174 feet (53 metres) high, and forms a fine landmark. However, its late Gothic detailing is not very good. The inside of the nave and aisles is better, but the tall, Perpendicular-style piers have strange acanthus-leaves and abaci with the classical 'egg-and-dart' motif. Luckily, the medieval eastern arm of the church is still intact and contains some much finer architecture.

There was an Anglo-Saxon church here, but in the early 12th century, the first earls of Warwick, Henry de Newburgh, and his son, Roger, rebuilt the church as a collegiate church. This was completed in 1123, and some impressive remains of this building survive under the chancel in the crypt, including large piers with scalloped capitals and heavy rib-vaults.

By the mid-14th century, the Beauchamp family had become the earls of Warwick and Thomas, who died in 1369, was one of the first Knights of the Garter. His son, another Thomas,

rebuilt the chancel with his parents' tomb at its centre; their fine effigies can be seen on a magnificent Purbeck marble tomb-chest. The rebuilding work was complete by 1392, and the great panelled interior of the chancel is a masterful example of early Perpendicular architecture. The tierceron vault, with its remarkable flying ribs, is the climax of the whole structure.

To the north of the chancel a chapel, which is now a vestry space, was built and flanked by a semi-octagonal chapter house for the meetings of the dean and chapter of the college. The college was dissolved at the Reformation, and the chapter house now contains the vast tomb of Fulke Greville, the first Lord Brooke, who died in 1628.

The most magnificent space in the whole church is the wonderful south-eastern chapel, known as the Beauchamp Chantry. It was constructed for Richard, the 13th Earl of Warwick (1382–1439), who was fabulously wealthy. He died at Rouen, where he was governor of France and Normandy under Henry VI – earlier he had been the king's tutor. This chantry, which was built between 1443 and 1464, cost almost £2,500 – a huge sum for the time. It was dedicated in 1475, the year in which the new monarch, Edward IV (1461–83), started his own extraordinary chantry chapel at St George's, Windsor. The chapel is superbly detailed, and at its centre is the amazing gilt-bronze effigy of Richard, covered by the unique gilt-bronze frame of his funeral car. The chapel also contains several other fine later tombs, including that of Robert Dudley, Earl of Leicester (1532–88), who was a favourite of Elizabeth I (1559–1603).

ABOVE: *The large Beauchamp chantry chapel contains Richard Beauchamp's fabulous tomb at its centre. Behind Richard Beauchamp is the very grand wall monument to Robert and Lettice Dudley.*

THE SOUTH-EAST

There is little good building stone in the south-east, so it was usually imported from elsewhere, particularly Caen in Normandy. The area does, however, contain a wonderful variety of parish churches, from by far the oldest in England in Canterbury to a completely new 19th-century church (made with money from pills) at Eastbourne. There are some very important Anglo-Saxon survivals and a unique very early Norman church with a chapel in the upper stage of its very strong west tower. The region also has two of the best 13th-century churches in England and some fascinating 'family' churches.

OPPOSITE: *The mural of Christ in Glory was made in 1888 for the high wall above the chancel arch in St Saviour's, Eastbourne.*

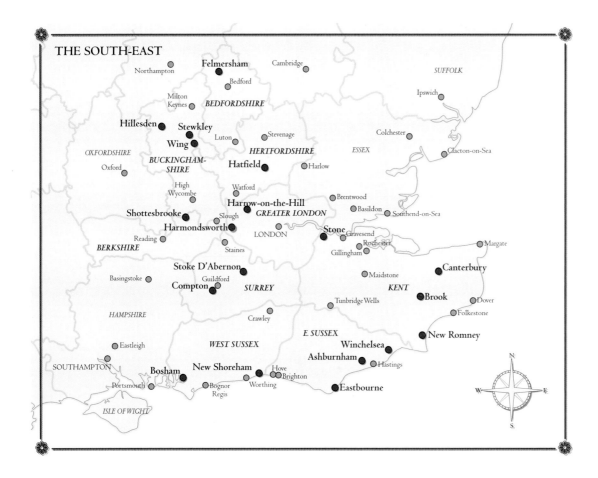

THE SOUTH-EAST

Northampton
Felmersham
Cambridge
SUFFOLK
Bedford
Ipswich
Milton Keynes
BEDFORDSHIRE
Hillesden
Stewkley
Luton
Stevenage
Colchester
Wing
HERTFORDSHIRE
ESSEX
Clacton-on-Sea
OXFORDSHIRE
BUCKINGHAM-SHIRE
Hatfield
Harlow
Oxford
High Wycombe
Watford
Harrow-on-the-Hill
Brentwood
Shottesbrooke
Slough
GREATER LONDON
Basildon
Southend-on-Sea
Harmondsworth
LONDON
Stone
Gravesend
Margate
BERKSHIRE
Reading
Staines
Rochester
Gillingham
Stoke D'Abernon
Maidstone
Canterbury
Basingstoke
Guildford
SURREY
KENT
Compton
Tunbridge Wells
Brook
Dover
HAMPSHIRE
Crawley
Folkestone
E. SUSSEX
New Romney
Eastleigh
WEST SUSSEX
Winchelsea
Ashburnham
SOUTHAMPTON
Bosham
New Shoreham
Hove
Hastings
Portsmouth
Bognor Regis
Worthing
Brighton
Eastbourne
ISLE OF WIGHT

HOLY TRINITY, BOSHAM

SUSSEX

osham is the oldest documented Christian site in Sussex. The Venerable Bede (*c.* 672–735), who wrote the *Ecclesiastical History of the English People* (AD 731), tells us that there were already Irish monks among the pagan South Saxons of Bosham when St Wilfrid (*c.* 633–709) arrived in the region in AD 681. The building also has the unique distinction of being the only English parish church depicted on the Bayeux Tapestry. This is because Harold Godwinson, the last Anglo-Saxon king of England, came here to pray with his soldiers, before setting out on his ill-fated diplomatic voyage to Normandy in the spring of 1064. Two years later, Harold was killed at the Battle of Hastings.

The tower and west end of the nave had almost certainly already been built when Harold came here, perhaps by his father Earl Godwin, but the very fine chancel arch was probably constructed a few years afterwards. At the time of the Norman Conquest, Bosham was one of Harold's many large estates, but it passed to William the Conqueror, who gave much land to one of his Norman priests, Osbern. He became Bishop of Exeter in 1072 and gave the church to future bishops of that diocese. His successor, Bishop William Warelwast, who began the construction of Norman Exeter Cathedral, probably enlarged the chancel at Bosham in the early 12th century and established a new college of six priests here. The chancel was expanded again in the early 13th century with a beautiful early Gothic east end. This allowed the six priests more room for their stalls in the western part of the chancel.

A north aisle was added to the nave in the late 12th century, but the south aisle does not seem to have been built until the 14th century. Remarkably, the outer walls of this aisle are made with stone from the Mixen Reef, which is situated off Selsey Bill. The reef is now only visible at low tide, but in the medieval period it may have been joined to Selsey by a shingle bank.

The south aisle is remarkable because it contains, beneath its east end, a vaulted crypt, which now forms a modern chapel. This aisle probably contained a chantry for Thomas of Brotherton, Earl of Norfolk (1300–1338), the son of Edward I by his second wife, Margaret of France. The chantry was founded in 1330, which is perhaps

when the aisle was started. At the completion of all this work in the church, Bishop John Grandison of Exeter re-dedicated the high altar in 1354. This very important bishop was also responsible for rebuilding the wonderful nave of Exeter Cathedral and for the superb church at Ottery St Mary in Devon (see pages 24–5).

Bosham's church was heavily restored in several stages in the later 19th century by the Reverend Henry Mitchell, who was vicar for nearly sixty years between 1845 and 1902. He stripped all the plaster, lowered the floor and renewed the roofs. He also uncovered a grave at the east end of the nave, which he claimed, erroneously, was that of King Canute's daughter.

ABOVE: *The fine early 13th-century east windows can be seen through the late 11th-century chancel arch.*

ST MARY DE HAURA, NEW SHOREHAM

SUSSEX

I n the late Anglo-Saxon period, the primary town on the River Adur, which was earlier called the Bramber, was on the west bank at Steyning. After the Norman Conquest, a large part of this area of Sussex, which consisted of thirty-eight manors, was assigned to the powerful lord, William de Braose. He built a castle at nearby Bramber, with a feudal town attached to it, and a little later gave the churches in the area to the Abbey of St Florent at Saumur in France. Among these churches was St Nicholas at Old Shoreham, which was on the east bank of the river near its estuary. A fine church still survives there with a late Anglo-Saxon nave and early 12th-century transepts and crossing tower. Before the end of the 11th century, however, the port had moved a little further down the river, and a new settlement was created around the church of St Mary de Haura – the name means haven or harbour. During the 12th century, this quickly became a new town and it was spectacularly successful as a cross-channel port. In about 1096, Philip, son of William de Braose, also gave St Mary de Haura to the Abbey of St Florent.

No sign of the earliest church can be seen because it was replaced from about 1130 by one of the most magnificent Romanesque parish churches in the whole of the south-east of England. As at Old Shoreham, the new work started with a relatively modest new crossing and transepts, but this very soon developed into a much more elaborate building with clerestories in the transepts and a large aisled nave. East of the transepts was a series of apsidal chapels, but by about 1170 work began on the lower outer walls of the very large aisled eastern arm. Large quantities of Caen stone were imported from Normandy, as well as several teams of very skilled stone masons, whose work must have overlapped during the next thirty or so years. The style of architecture in the arcades and triforia on the north and south sides of the building are quite different but typify the ideas of the earliest Gothic or 'Transitional' style of France and England.

As the work progressed it became even more ambitious, and stone quadripartite vaults were put into all parts of the eastern arm, thus necessitating the addition of large flying buttresses to the outsides. This all reflects the huge prosperity of the port of New Shoreham at this time. By the early 13th century the church was complete, and was situated at the centre of one of the most important ports on the south coast of England.

This situation did not last for more than a couple of centuries because in the 15th century the borough was 'greatly wasted by the sea and the inhabitants much impoverished thereby'. The most dramatic evidence for this was the destruction of the parish church's nave. Today, only a ruined fragment of the west wall in the churchyard survives to show the extent of the original nave. At its east end, however, the blocked up arches leading into the nave aisles can still be seen. There is also a Perpendicular window in the shortened west wall, and nearby small, yellow, late medieval bricks can be seen in the quoins.

The chequer-work masonry on the lower north-west corner of Shoreham's magnificent two-storey, 12th-century tower, is probably the result of repairs in the 16th century.

BELOW: *New Shoreham's crossing tower is a splendid piece of Romanesque architecture. Note also the late 12th-century flying buttress supporting the chancel vault.*

ST SAVIOUR AND ST PETER, EASTBOURNE

SUSSEX

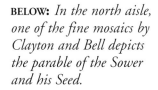

ABOVE: *The large tower and spire over the porch dominate the red-brick church.*

BELOW: *In the north aisle, one of the fine mosaics by Clayton and Bell depicts the parable of the Sower and his Seed.*

The town of Eastbourne, which lies at the foot of Beachy Head, started to become a fashionable bathing-place after the railway arrived in the mid-19th century and development of the new town subsequently began. The chief landowner, the 7th Duke of Devonshire, was the primary developer. Over the next half-century a welter of townhouses and several churches were built. Only one of these churches, St Saviour and St Peter's (which is generally known simply by its original dedication of St Saviour) stands out. It is a fine, late Victorian Gothic church and still dominates the area. The architect was G.E. Street (1824–81), and his fine brick church is a most imposing building, with a great steeple porch at its north-west corner.

The money for the new church came largely from George Whelpton of Louth, a wealthy manufacturer of pills. Whelpton insisted that his son, Henry, should be the first vicar. The main body of the church was constructed between 1865 and 1867 and Henry Robert Whelpton served the parish for the next thirty years, to be followed by his son, Henry Urling Whelpton, who was also vicar for thirty years. Initially, the church was a 'district chaplery' to the old parish church of St Mary, but in 1892 it received full parochial status, with the Whelptons named as

patrons of the living. In 1943, this patronage was transferred to Keble College, Oxford.

Street's design mimics the style of the late 13th century. He created a tall nave and aisles, with a vaulted chancel and apse. Over the nave is a large clerestory, with an Italianate boarded wagon roof above it. The 175-foot (52-metre) tall broach spire was finally finished in 1872. However, the adornment of the interior continued for the next half century.

The decoration of the brickwork of the upper side walls is still to be completed, but at the east end of the nave, which converges inwards, and above the very large chancel arch is a fine painting depicting Christ in Glory (see pages 98–9). This was painted in 1888 by Clayton and Bell and was well restored in 1991. The painted work was continued on either side of the church in 1890 with four figures representing the 'Doctors of the Church' – Saints Ambrose, Jerome, Gregory, and Augustine of Hippo – dominating the upper east walls. In 1896, a baptistry was added to the west end of the nave, and this contains a font crafted from Mexican onyx and designed by Street. It is surrounded by mosaics of St Augustine preaching to King Ethelbert and of King Oswald of Northumbria setting up the cross at Heavenfield.

Around the aisle walls are a fine set of mosaics, also designed by Clayton and Bell, and many hours could be spent looking at the different scenes depicted. Sadly, much of the Victorian glass was destroyed by wartime bombing.

ABOVE: *The elaborate 1937 reredos above the high altar was a memorial to the Reverend H.U. Whelpton, who died in 1927.*

LEFT: *The mosaics in the niches around the chancel, including this image of St John the Baptist and the Lamb of God, were designed by Clayton and Bell and made by Salviati of Venice.*

ST PETER, ASHBURNHAM
SUSSEX

ABOVE: *The view down the nave to the 17th-century gallery. The contemporary font is on the right.*

BELOW: *John Bushnell created a superb memorial to William and Jane Ashburnham, who was also Countess of Marlborough.*

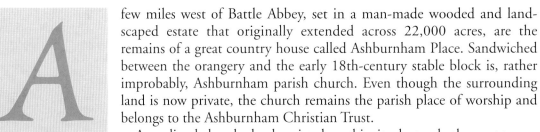

A few miles west of Battle Abbey, set in a man-made wooded and landscaped estate that originally extended across 22,000 acres, are the remains of a great country house called Ashburnham Place. Sandwiched between the orangery and the early 18th-century stable block is, rather improbably, Ashburnham parish church. Even though the surrounding land is now private, the church remains the parish place of worship and belongs to the Ashburnham Christian Trust.

A medieval church clearly existed on this site, but only the west tower, which dates from the 15th century, survives. The rest of the building was completely rebuilt between 1663 and 1665, although some of the earlier window tracery and internal arches were reused. The man who paid for all this work was John Ashburnham (1603–1671), who suffered greatly during the period of the Civil War and Commonwealth, when he was fined and imprisoned. With the Restoration in 1660, everything changed, and John Ashburnham, who had been

Groom of the Bedchamber to Charles I, resumed his life at court under Charles II (1660–85). He built a magnificent house in London, which still survives just to the south of the cloister at Westminster Abbey, while at Ashburnham Place he constructed an impressive country house (sadly demolished half a century ago).

At the same time, Ashburnham took down the walls of the parish church and had it rebuilt for his own use and that of the parishioners. The whole of the new eastern arm, which had originally been a chancel flanked by two chapels, was made into a large and primarily subterranean burial vault. Over this a new chancel was constructed, which was flanked by a chamber to the north for family memorials. The family pew was on the south side, and had its own separate doorway, a fireplace and stairs to the pew itself, which was in an upper gallery.

Remarkably, many of the late 17th-century fittings for this church still survive, the most magnificent being the memorials to John Ashburnham and his brother, William, who died in 1679. John's memorial is medieval in form, and is a recumbent effigy that shows him

dressed in armour and lying between his two wives. On the front of the 'tomb' are reliefs of his sons and daughters. By contrast, William's memorial is completely Baroque in style. Its sculptor, John Bushnell, who was trained in Italy, created a tableau that showed William kneeling before his dying wife, Jane, Countess of Marlborough. Behind these sculptures is a drapery canopy with putti.

In the chancel, the late 17th-century communion rail survives. The pedimented Table of Commandments (Decalogue), which once sat behind the Communion Table, is now situated on the south side of the nave. It dates from 1676 and features painted figures of Moses and Aaron on either side. The box pews are still in the nave and were cut down to their present size in 1893, while at the western end of the church is a fine gallery, which stands on large Ionic columns and is accessed by a proper 'domestic' staircase in the tower. There is also a contemporary font, with a large stem and white marble bowl, and a panelled pulpit. Wrought-iron screens, which were made at the Ashburnham furnace, survive in the tower, chancel and chapels.

ABOVE: *The 15th-century west tower is the only part of the church to date from before the Reformation; everything beyond it was built in the 1660s.*

ST THOMAS, WINCHELSEA

SUSSEX

ABOVE: *A queen's head sits above the medieval tomb of Stephen Alard.*

BELOW: *The ruined transepts are still dominant in St Thomas's graveyard.*

The old town of Winchelsea, which was situated at the extreme eastern end of Sussex, was destroyed by the sea in 1287. In its place, a prestigious new town, planned around a grid like Salisbury, was created by Edward I on a hilltop a few miles to the north. A magnificent parish church was built within the centre of one of the new town's blocks (or quarters). This great church was cruciform and surrounded by a large, 3-acre churchyard. It had a long, aisled chancel and a crossing with transepts. Today, only the chancel survives from the original church, but its wonderful Decorated architecture tells us that it was built between the very end of the 13th century and the beginning of the 14th century.

There has been some debate over whether the church was ever completed, and until archaeological excavations are carried out this cannot be resolved. However, the town was initially very successful, and documentary evidence shows that there was a large population at Winchelsea in the early 14th century. This strongly suggests that the whole church would have been completed

before the devastating raids on the town by the French in 1337, 1359–60 and 1380, and the appalling results of the Black Death, which ravaged England in 1348–9.

In the later Middle Ages depopulation continued, caused mainly by the silting of the town's harbour, and the retreat of the sea from the town. By the time of the Reformation, Winchelsea was only sparsely inhabited. In the 16th century the nave was probably demolished and the south-west tower came down only in the 18th century. A new west porch to the chancel was built. Although the ruined shells of the transepts survive, they may have been unroofed earlier.

Inside the surviving chancel, architecture of the highest quality dating from the years around 1300 can be seen. There is much use of stone imported from Caen, which is carved with elaborate Decorated tracery. The compound piers still have fine, dark shafts, capitals and bases of Purbeck marble. More Purbeck marble was used for string-courses and internal shafts around the windows.

In the side walls of the aisles are set five of the finest early 14th-century canopied tombs in England. Recent scholarship has, at last, revealed the names of their occupants. The north aisle originally featured an altar dedicated to St Nicholas at the east end. It was here that Robert Alard, who died in 1328, founded a chantry in 1319 'for the souls of Henry Alard, my uterine brother, Isabel my dead wife, and for my own'. The three splendid Purbeck marble effigies here, of a knight, lady, and a beardless young man, are clearly Robert Alard, his wife and brother. On the south, where a chantry was founded in the Lady chapel by Stephen Alard in 1312, are the even more magnificent tombs and Caen stone effigies of Stephen Alard and Sir William Maufe. The latter has a shield with his coat of arms on it.

There is much bright, but streaky, stained glass in the church, which was designed by Douglas Strachan between 1928 and 1933.

ST NICHOLAS, NEW ROMNEY

KENT

ABOVE: *A fine brass in the Lady chapel shows Thomas Smyth (died 1611) and his family.*

T he little town of New Romney is now a mile or so inland from the sea on the south-eastern side of Romney Marsh. In the 12th century, however, it was the site of a busy port. This haven was so important that a major canal, now called the Rhee Wall, was built in the 13th century to stop the haven silting up. The parish church, too, was greatly affected by the sea, and its eastern arm was probably wrecked by the great storm of 1287, which also covered large areas of the town in sand and shingle. This is most noticeable at the building's western end, where it is obvious that the modern ground level is several feet above the 12th-century ground level.

The early history of the church is intimately tied up with its patron, the Archbishop of Canterbury. The western part of the large aisled nave was constructed in the mid-12th century, and Thomas Becket would have seen it when he tried unsuccessfully to sail out of New Romney in 1164. At this time, work had begun on a large new western tower, but the murder of Becket in 1170 must have halted this.

Work continued in the 1180s, but once again, the tower did not reach completion. At the end of the 12th century, the structure was finally completed and work started on a stone spire, but this was probably left unfinished during the interdict in the later part of the reign of King John (1199–1216). The spire was finally finished during Archbishop Stephen Langton's (*c.* 1156–1228) time, but it seems to have collapsed

RIGHT: *The Lady chapel on the north side of the chancel has fine reticulated window tracery.*

RIGHT: *A window in the south aisle commemorates those who drowned when the ship* Northfleet *foundered off the coast near New Romney in January 1873.*

BELOW: *The large, early 14th-century eastern arm is seen here in the foreground, with the great west tower with its cut-off spire beyond.*

in the 15th century, after which it was left in its present curtailed form.

After the great storms of the late 13th century, the nave aisles were rebuilt on a larger scale, but once again the work seems to have been left incomplete for some time. Finally, in the early 14th century, the magnificent new eastern arm was built, terminating in the row of three large gable-ends of the chancel and its flanking chapels of Our Lady and St Stephen.

The east windows are all filled with reticulated tracery, while inside the building the fine arcades, the aisle windows and altar fittings are beautiful examples of Decorated architecture. The original roofs also survive here.

The decline of the town in the later Middle Ages and beyond was reflected by the church. No new architectural work was carried out, although the interior is filled with some fascinating later fittings. A drastic restoration was started on the Romanesque work on the north side of the nave in 1880, but the vicar was forced to stop after pressure from the newly founded Society for the Protection of Ancient Buildings. The magnificent tower, how-ever, is still a fine landmark on the edge of Romney Marsh, and a seamark from the English Channel to the east. Nearby is the famous Romney, Hythe and Dymchurch miniature railway.

ST MARY, BROOK

KENT

ust below the North Downs, a little over 3 miles (5km) north-east of the new international railway station at Ashford, is the remarkable early Norman church of St Mary at Brook. This building was probably first constructed in the 1080s by Archbishop Lanfranc (*c.* 1010–89), who had acquired the manor of Brook for his monks at Canterbury. The church and manor continued to belong to the priory at Canterbury Cathedral until the Dissolution of the Monasteries in the 16th century, after which it was passed on to the new dean and chapter of Canterbury. As a result of this, the church was as much a manorial church as a parish church and no new building work was attempted, apart from the insertion of a few windows.

The simple chancel and nave were the first parts of the church to be built in the 1080s, with local coursed flints used for the walls. However, all the quoins and the plain chancel arch were made with Quarr stone from the Isle of Wight. After the death of Archbishop Lanfranc, there was a period of instability under King William Rufus (1087–1100), and it was probably at this time that the west wall of the nave was pulled down and the massive, squat and strongly built west

ABOVE: *A roundel depicting the Magi with Herod on the south side of the chancel.*

BELOW: *The strong and foreboding late 11th-century tower of St Mary's church, as seen from the north-west.*

113

tower was erected. The quoins in this part of the church are largely made from Caen stone. The west tower has its own spiral staircase, which at the first-floor level leads to a private chapel, containing the remains of its original stone altar. Above the altar, in a niche in the east wall, is a Romanesque painting of Christ in Majesty.

The church contains some remarkable wall paintings, most of which date from the 13th century. They were probably painted before the lancet windows were installed in the chancel and the piscina and sedilia were made. The wall paintings are in rows of roundels, which once continued all round the inside of the chancel. In the nave are larger roundels on the south wall, and various other later medieval figures, including St Christopher, can be seen above the north door, which is in part covered over by 17th-century texts in large cartouches.

To the south of the church is the late medieval court lodge, the name used in Kent for an ecclesiastical manor house, and in its farm-yard is a magnificent 14th-century great barn, which now houses an agricultural museum.

BELOW: *These 13th-century wall paintings appear on the 11th-century chancel walls; the wide lancets were inserted after the paintings had been made.*

ST MARTIN, CANTERBURY

KENT

 his small parish church, which is situated outside Canterbury's eastern city walls, is famous because it can justifiably claim to have maintained the longest continuous use of any church in Britain. The Venerable Bede tells us that 'on the east side of the city stood an old church, built in honour of St Martin during the Roman occupation of Britain, where the Christian queen of whom I have spoken [Bertha, wife of King Ethelbert] went to pray. Here they first assembled to sing psalms, to pray, to say Mass, to preach and to baptise, until the King's own conversion to the Faith gave them greater freedom to preach and to build and restore churches everywhere.'

The western part of the chancel, which can best be seen outside the church on the south side, is made of large, broken Roman bricks and other reused Roman materials. It was built either in the late Roman period or in the 6th century. On its south side is an original doorway, which was covered by a large, flat lintel that was possibly once a Roman grave-marker. This door leads into another chamber; however, it was probably blocked up in the 7th century, when a new round-headed doorway was inserted into the wall just to the east.

The nave of the church, which survives to its full height, was constructed in the 7th century after St Augustine and his monks, who arrived here in AD 597, had built their monastery nearby. The nave walls are of a distinctive masonry, made with small blockwork of local sandstone and string-courses of Roman brick, all set in a pink Roman mortar that was made from crushed

ABOVE: *The lower part of the chancel wall, with its blocked doorways, may well date from as far back as the 6th century, and contains reused Roman materials.*

BELOW: *The east end of Canterbury cathedral can be seen in the distance from the churchyard of St Martin's church.*

bricks. Inside the nave, the plaster has been removed from the west wall, and the masonry indicates the positions of the original round-headed windows on either side, each of which was extended upwards, probably in the later Anglo-Saxon period. The windows were blocked up at the end of the 14th century when the west tower and porch were built.

Before the Norman Conquest, this was an important church, and contained the seat for the suffragan (subordinate) bishop to the Archbishop of Canterbury. At the end of the 11th century, St Martin's became an ordinary parish church, and it has remained so ever since. In the 13th century, the chancel was lengthened eastwards, but remarkably the nave was never enlarged with aisles, leaving its 7th-century walls largely intact, although a few later medieval windows were inserted. The roof of the nave is late 14th-century, and was put in when the west tower was built.

At the end of the 19th century, the church was restored and the internal walls were stripped of plaster. At this time, there was much heated debate about the exact age of the walls. The remarkable mid-12th-century font was not built as a font, but perhaps as a well-head. It may have been moved here from Canterbury Cathedral priory just after the Reformation.

ABOVE: *The early 7th-century west wall of the nave has its original doorway filled in. The upper masonry is part of the tower and dates from the 14th century.*

ABOVE RIGHT: *This mid-12th-century font was originally a well-head in the cathedral priory.*

ST MARY, STONE

KENT

This, the finest 13th-century church in Kent, is prominently situated on a hillside beside the River Thames that overlooks the Queen Elizabeth Bridge on the Dartford crossing of the M25. Until recently, the area to the south was covered in vast, derelict chalk pits, which were remnants of the local cement industry. The area now contains much new housing and the huge Bluewater shopping centre. In the Middle Ages, the main road from London to Canterbury and Dover (now the A226) ran across the parish just quarter of a mile (0.4km) to the south of the church. Immediately to the west of the church was a large manorial residence for the bishops of Rochester. It must have been two of the bishops, Richard of Wendene (1238–50) and Laurence of St Martin (1251–74), who constructed this exceptionally fine building.

The earliest part of the church is the beautifully proportioned three-bay, aisled nave, whose architectural decoration gets progressively more elaborate as one moves eastwards. At first sight it is more like the aisled great hall of a major palace. Only the finest materials are used, including

ABOVE: *The 14th-century west end of the church has a 15th-century top stage to its tower.*

ABOVE RIGHT: *The vault and windows in the chancel were restored by the Victorian architect G.E. Street, but the superb blind arcading below dates from the 1250s.*

Caen and Reigate stone and Purbeck marble. Just beyond the beautifully carved chancel arch is the start of a narrower chancel, but after only a few feet it opens out into an amazing rib-vaulted chancel that has at its lower level very elaborate, carved arcading, exactly like that found in Westminster Abbey. How this similarity came about is not certain; however, when Bishop Richard died in 1250 he was buried in Westminster Abbey when Henry III was beginning to build the eastern arm of his new abbey.

The window tracery and stone vaults in the chancel were restored between 1859 and 1860 by the Victorian architect G.E. Street, who had good archaeological evidence to follow. The

earlier vault was destroyed in 1640. At the west end of the nave, an aisled extension and a tower were built in about 1300, but this structure was not completed until the 15th century, when the present upper stage of the tower was built. It once had a spire on it, but this came down in 1638.

Externally, Street's major restoration is fairly noticeable, but inside one still sees the exceptionally splendid early Gothic architecture. In 1526, a small chantry chapel, with a flying buttress constructed over it, was built on the north side of the chancel for the Wiltshyre family; it still contains a fine early Tudor family wall-tomb.

ST MARY, STOKE D'ABERNON

SURREY

This church became famous because it was thought to contain within it 'the oldest brass in England', that of Sir John d'Abernon, who died in 1277. Alas, modern scholarship tells us that this magnificent brass and its equally fine neighbour both date from the early 14th century and actually commemorate Sir John's son and grandson. The second Sir John, who died in 1327, entertained King Edward I at his manor house, which is just to the east of the church, in May 1305. His splendid brass is superbly made. The figure holds a 6-foot (1.8-metre) long lance and has a heraldic shield that is coloured with blue Limoges enamel.

The church itself lies beside the River Mole, close to the manor and away from the village. It is a beautiful spot, although slightly marred by the noise of the M25, which is situated to the south. Until a major rebuilding and enlargement of the nave in 1866, most of the shell of the original late Anglo-Saxon building survived, as early 19th-century pictures displayed in the church show. The south wall of the nave still displays quite a lot of its Anglo-Saxon fabric. Much rarer is the survival of parts of the curved north and south walls of the small Anglo-Saxon apsidal sanctuary. This is best seen above the later vault, under the chancel roof, although part of the early wall can also be seen in the Norbury Chapel.

At the end of the 12th century, a north aisle was added to the nave, and the two pointed arches leading into this still survive, as does the eastern round pier with its moulded capital and spurred base. In the early 13th century, the centre of the apse was knocked out and a very fine new chancel was built. Most unusually, this is covered by two bays of quadripartite stone vaulting, the ribs of which extend onto capitals, shafts and bases that stand on an internal wall-bench. The present three-light '13th-century' east window was actually made in the 19th century, replacing the earlier 14th-century one.

The last addition to the medieval church was the Norbury Chapel on the

ABOVE: *The 17th-century pulpit is a fine example of carving skills.*

BELOW: *The 1866 tower and spire sit seamlessly beside the older church.*

ABOVE: *The tomb of Lady Sarah Vincent, who died in 1608. Above her and to the right is the later memorial (a kneeling figure) to Sir John Norbury.*

RIGHT: *A detail from the superb brass of Sir John d'Abernon, who died in 1327.*

north-east side of the building. This was constructed in the 1490s by Sir John Norbury, a veteran of the famous Battle of Bosworth Field in 1485, who died in 1521. His tomb was built into a wide opening in the wall between the chapel and the chancel, but was destroyed in the 16th century. The Vincents, who were descendants of Norbury, and owned the manor in the early 17th century, are commemorated by some fine monuments in the chapel. They also commissioned the kneeling figure of their esteemed ancestor. Near the north-west corner of the Norbury Chapel is an original fireplace, which would have kept the chantry-priests warm, while on the south-west is a stair-turret to the contemporary rood loft, which is in front of the chancel arch; the original rood screen and loft have sadly been destroyed.

The church also contains many fine 17th-century fittings, including a splendid seven-sided pulpit, with an hour-glass on the wall nearby.

ST NICHOLAS, COMPTON
SURREY

 ituated just to the south of the Hog's Back, the narrow chalk ridge between Farnham and Guildford, is one of the most interesting churches in Surrey. The church has a unique feature – a two-storey sanctuary at its eastern end with a stone rib-vault over the lower sanctuary. No satisfactory reason has yet been found for this, and originally the upper sanctuary can only have been accessible by a ladder.

The building displays a clear sequence of enlargement, which took place over a period of about 100 years, starting with the western tower and west end of the nave, which were built in the 11th century. The church is mentioned in Domesday Book, but we do not know for certain if it was built before the Norman Conquest, or whether the tower and nave were constructed soon after this.

In the 12th century, as happens with so many churches, aisles were added to the nave to provide more room for the rapidly expanding population of the parish. At this point there were no pews, so the congregation stood for the services. Compton's aisles are still entered through three very slightly pointed arches on either side, which were installed during the latter part of the 12th century. There are also some fine round pillars with beautifully carved capitals that are made from local chalk. In the lower, outer walls of the aisles one can see some of the original round-headed windows and a fine southern doorway. In the 15th century, when the pews were first put in position, the aisle walls were heightened slightly and much larger Perpendicular windows were inserted. At the same time, the roof was rebuilt, and a fine broached spire was put on top of the tower.

The original 11th-century east end of the church would have been a small, roughly square sanctuary enclosing the main altar. In the later 12th century, at about the same time as the aisles were being built, the east wall of the church was removed and the remarkable two-storey sanctuary was built, along with a new chancel arch. The enlarged east end contains a thickly walled quadripartite rib-vault, below which is a small contemporary window. The upper storey of the sanctuary is now entered via a relatively modern wooden staircase that is placed in the very small 14th-century chantry chapel on the south side of the chancel. It has its own altar and, rather strangely, the upper sanctuary is now lit only from above by dormer windows. Before 1953, however, there was a sequence of upper east windows, the last of which was made in 1859. A unique feature of the upper sanctuary is the late 12th-century timber screen on its west side.

FOLLOWING PAGE: *The church features a shingled broach spire on an 11th-century tower.*

ABOVE: *Fragments of a 13th-century Virgin and Child have been reset in the east window.*

BELOW: *St Nicholas's has a remarkable two-storeyed chancel.*

ST MARY, HARROW-ON-THE-HILL

LONDON

ABOVE: *Detail of the late 17th-century pulpit.*

BELOW: *The interior of Elias's 13th-century church includes nave walls that were raised and given a new roof in the 15th century.*

arrow, which is now best known for its famous school, was at the centre of a very large group of estates that were acquired by the Archbishop of Canterbury in AD 825. It remained in the hands of successive archbishops, and was surrendered to Henry VIII only in 1545. The church is splendidly situated on the top of the eponymous hill at 400 feet (122 metres) above sea level, and its octagonal spire can be seen for miles around.

The oldest visible part of the church is the west tower, which dates from the middle of the 12th century, and was no doubt added to the nave of an earlier church – it is very likely that there was a major Anglo-Saxon place of worship on the site. In the north and

IOANNI · LION
PRESTONIAE · IN · PAROECIA · HARROVIENSI
MORTVO
SEXT · NON · OCTOBR · ANNO · CHRISTI · MDXCII
ET · IN · HAC · ECCLESIA · SEPVLTO
FVNDI · DOMINO · CVLTORI · QVE
ASSIDVO · FRVGI · PROBO
SAPIENTI · SINE · VIA · ET · ARTE
ET · QVIA · BONIS · SVIS · OPTIME · VTI · NOVIT
VNICE · FORTVNATO
SCHOLAE · IMPENSIS · EIVS · EXTRVCTAE
ET · AD · PVEROS · GRAECIS · AC · LATINIS · LITTERIS
ERVDIENDOS · INSTITVTAE
GVBERNATORES · MAGISTRI · ATQVE · ALVMNI
HOC · MONIMENTVM · COLLATA · PECVNIA
PONENDVM · CVRAVERVNT
ANNO · SACRO · MDCCCXV.

ABOVE: *The tall tower and spire sit atop Harrow Hill. Most of the visible exterior of the church is now mid-19th-century knapped flintwork.*

ABOVE RIGHT: *The 1815 monument to John Lyon by Flaxman sits on the north side of the nave.*

south walls of the tower are two medieval windows that are deeply splayed inside, and there is also a fine west doorway with chevron decoration.

At some time early in the 13th century, a famous man, Master Elias of Dereham, was made Rector of Harrow. He worked for several archbishops, and was heavily involved with the Magna Carta in 1215. In 1220, he also became a canon of Salisbury, and was in charge of building the new cathedral on the site for some 25 years. At Harrow, Elias was responsible for the rebuilding of the church in its present form, with the exception of the west tower. The church was

constructed with a new four-bay aisled nave, transepts and large chancel. One fragment of documentary evidence tells us that Elias acquired timber for the chancel in 1242, but unfortunately the chancel was rebuilt between 1846 and 1849, and little of the earlier work survives.

The aisle walls and the transepts were rebuilt in the early 14th century, and the nave was given a clerestory and fine new roof in the 15th century. Sadly, the most obvious thing about the church today is the very heavy restoration work that was carried out by George Gilbert Scott in the 1840s. Apart from rebuilding the chancel, he added the north porch, rebuilt the south porch and re-faced the exterior (with the exception of the tower) in heavy non-medieval knapped flint. He also added the large north-east chapel and the vestry.

Inside the church is a fine late 12th-century Purbeck marble font, as well as an excellent series of brasses in the chancel floor, including two that are dedicated to a pair of late 14th-century knights. There is also a small brass commemorating the founder of Harrow School, John Lyon (1514–92), and his wife.

ST MARY, HARMONDSWORTH

MIDDLESEX

 ess than a mile from the main runway of Heathrow Airport, and threatened with demolition owing to the proposed third runway of the airport, lies this fascinating little church. It is still situated within a small village, and remarkably still has fields to the north and west, albeit bordered by the M4 and M25. Immediately to the west of the churchyard are the remains of the manor farm, which was once owned by Winchester College. Within the disused farmyard is a granary on staddle stones and one of the largest surviving great barns in England, which was built for the college in the 1420s. It is often wrongly described as a tithe barn.

The church itself is still, to a certain extent, hidden among the yew trees of the churchyard, although its striking early Tudor brick tower rises above them. Entering the church through the south porch next to the tower, visitors are immediately confronted by a magnificent mid-12th-century doorway. Although such architecture is now rare in Middlesex, there is another fine

12th-century doorway at nearby Harlington Church. The doorway is made of Barnack stone, which comes from the edge of the Fens, and it seems to have been reset in the later Middle Ages, when the south aisle of the church was rebuilt and re-roofed – the fine 15th-century roof survives. The late medieval roofs also survive over the nave and chancel, although they were quite heavily restored in 1862.

The nave of the church has aisles on either side, which reached their present form in the 13th century, although, somewhat unusually, the southern arcade has mid-12th-century piers that are made of Barnack and Reigate stone, with scalloped

ABOVE: *Harmondsworth church and the local village green form an amazing oasis of calm in an otherwise busy area close to Heathrow Airport.*

BELOW: *The large aisled nave has 12th-century carved capitals in the south arcade.*

ABOVE: *The 16th-century brick south-west tower, atop of which is an open 18th-century cupola.*

capitals. The pointed arches above them were certainly added in the 13th century.

The wide chancel was rebuilt between 1396 and 1398 by Winchester College soon after it was given the manor by Bishop William of Wykeham (1324–1404), the institution's great founder. On the north side of the chancel is a manorial chapel, which was also originally built in the 14th century. This chapel, however, was

given a magnificent new miniature hammer-beam roof in the early 16th century, after a completely new arcade was made to the chancel. This has flat, four-centred arches, and the westernmost arch stops suddenly, almost certainly because it originally abutted a large new rood screen that has since disappeared. The church is also highly unusual in retaining a magnificent set of early Tudor pews.

ST JOHN, SHOTTESBROOKE

BERKSHIRE

This delightful little early 14th-century church, which now lies in a post-medieval parkland landscape, is situated just under 10 miles (16km) due west of Windsor. The church was built in the decade after 1335 for Sir William Trussell, who founded a small college of priests here in 1337, within the bounds of Windsor Forest. Trussell came from Staffordshire, but as a young man he had entered the household of Edward, Prince of Wales. In 1327, when the young prince became Edward III, Trussell automatically became an esquire of the royal household, and accompanied the monarch on many of his travels. He was a knight by 1335, and was constantly on active service at the beginning of the Hundred Years War. He also acquired the manor of Shottesbrooke in 1335, and quickly decided to build his new church here with a group of priests – a warden and five other chaplains – to pray for Trussell and his friends in life and for their souls after death. As a household knight to the king, he did quite well financially, but he never made a huge amount of money, so his church – compared to its contemporary at Patrington (see pages 215–17) is relatively modest. It is, however, a beautifully proportioned structure with a tall slender spire, and has been little altered since the mid-14th century.

The church is perfectly symmetrical and has a cruciform plan, with nave, chancel, transepts and north and south nave porches. There are no aisles, and the nave is a little smaller than the chancel, showing the relatively small population of the parish at this time. There is not a great deal of expensive decoration inside, but the windows, particularly the east window, have fine flowing Decorated tracery, and the splendid double tomb of Trussell and his wife, which can be found in the north transept, is a magnificent affair, replete with now-empty statue niches. Trussell survived the Black Death, living until 1363.

In the chancel, where the collegiate stalls once stood, there is a simple ogee-headed sedilia and a piscina, and many of the

ABOVE: *Corbel of a queen's head on the south-west crossing pier.*

BELOW: *The wonderful flowing Decorated tracery in the east window.*

windows still contain fragments of the original stained glass. There is also an excellent brass of about 1386 depicting a layman and a priest. This may represent William Frith, a London fishmonger and a relative of Trussell, who was one of the college priests. The tomb of one William Throckmorton, who was the penultimate warden of the college and who died in 1535, is in the north wall of the chancel. It is a remarkable alabaster figure of a moustached man in his coffin, with two large brass inscriptions running across the centre.

The college near the church disappeared in the 19th century. Nearby is 18th-century Shottesbrooke Park.

LEFT: *The perfectly symmetrical church has a slender spire and beautiful traceried east window.*

BELOW: *Sir William Trussell and his wife have a magnificent double tomb in the north transept.*

ALL SAINTS, WING

BUCKINGHAMSHIRE

 few miles north-west of the Chiltern scarp at Ivinghoe Beacon is one of the most complete Anglo-Saxon churches in England. It is also one of the most interesting, and in the later Middle Ages it remained a very fine parish church. Sadly, however, there is no documentary evidence to tell us about its foundation or construction.

The nave, aisles and very unusual polygonal chancel all date from the Anglo-Saxon period, though the south aisle walls were almost completely rebuilt in the early 14th century. This major Anglo-Saxon church was probably built in the 8th or early 9th century, and from the start it had three large arches on either side of the nave into the aisles; the eastern pointed arches date from the 13th century. The chancel is raised up on several steps, because beneath it is an Anglo-Saxon crypt. This was

ABOVE: *The Anglo-Saxon groin-vaulted crypt, looking south across the central relic chamber.*

RIGHT: *The sanctuary has a wide Anglo-Saxon arch with a two-light window above. The fine monument on the left of the picture is by Roubiliac, and it commemorates Henry Fiennes, who died in 1758.*

rediscovered and dug out again in 1881, and what remains is an exceptionally rare survival of a crypt with a central chamber for relics surrounded by an ambulatory.

The present entrance to the crypt is from the exterior of the chancel on the south, but as can still be seen inside, the original entrances were approached by stepped passageways from the eastern end of the nave into the ambulatory. The seven-sided exterior wall of the chancel still displays Anglo-Saxon decoration – thin pilaster strips at the angles, with semi-circular blind arcading above them and triangular gable-like shapes at the top. Inside the nave, a very wide Anglo-Saxon chancel arch can be seen, with a large two-light Anglo-Saxon window above it. The west end of the Anglo-Saxon nave was destroyed when the massive bell-tower was built in the 15th century, but the doorways to a west gallery still survive on either side.

In the late 15th century, major building work took place again at the church. Apart from the new west tower, the walls of the nave were heightened and given new clerestory windows. Above this is a beautiful angel roof, with a mass of splendid figures on either side, and great winged angels on the central trusses. A new south porch was also built and the eastern end of the south aisle was screened off as St Katherine's Chapel. Unusually, the west screen here had a small loft above it, which was entered from a tiny spiral staircase inserted into the wall. Another, larger, spiral staircase was built on the south side of the chancel arch, to give access to the rood loft.

The Lady chapel was at the east end of the north aisle, but most traces of this were removed during the Elizabethan period, when the magnificent classical monument was built here for Sir Robert Dormer, who died in 1552. Two more splendid monuments to the Dormer family were placed on either side of the chancel, outside of which is a Jacobean pulpit that dates from about 1620.

ST MICHAEL, STEWKLEY

BUCKINGHAMSHIRE

ABOVE: *An animal head capital in the south porch.*

Stewkley is only 3 miles (4.8km) north-west of the famous Anglo-Saxon church at Wing (see pages 129–30), although here we have a completely different church – a fine mid-12th-century parish church that has remained virtually intact since it was first built. Very unusually, no later enlargements have been made, even to the chancel. The church at Iffley near Oxford has a very similar plan to Stewkley: a large central tower flanked by a rectangular nave and square, rib-vaulted sanctuary; however, at Iffley the sanctuary was enlarged eastwards in the 13th century. Both churches have many similarities, including three doorways (north, west and south) at the western end of the nave, and similar chancel and sanctuary arches with all the decoration on the western sides. They also have similar late Romanesque carved decoration, although at Stewkley chevron patterns are dominant – even on the string-courses and window surrounds.

The most elaborate decoration is on the west front, which has been recently cleaned and restored. The west doorway, flanked by blind arches, has an unusual tympanum of dragons with curved tails, cut in two by a thin keystone.

Inside, the most important space, as always, was the eastern sanctuary, and this is marked by the splendid quadripartite rib-vault above it, and the capitals, shafts and bases in the corners. By the time of the first restoration of the church in 1844, the walls had been pushed out by the vault and new brick webbing had to be put in. The exterior pilaster buttresses also had to be rebuilt.

The main restoration took place in 1862, under G.E. Street, and the present interior furnishings of the church are largely his work. Street designed the pulpit and reredos and put in neat rows of pews and the new steep-pitched roof over the nave with a new round window in the west gable. Street also employed the well-known firm of Clayton and Bell to add the red-painted decoration to the sanctuary vault and to put in the stained glass in the east window.

BELOW: *Nineteenth-century buttressing supports the 12th-century vaulted sanctuary.*

While the restoration was being carried out, a fine 15th-century alabaster tablet was found in the wall. This shows the Virgin and Child with attendant angels, and still has much of the medieval polychromy. One other late medieval feature, the door halfway up on the wall on the north side of the chancel arch, is probably a last vestige of the rood screen and loft. Externally, the very top of the tower, replete with fine gargoyle spouts, is late medieval. Above these is a slim 1964 parapet, which replaced the more substantial affair with large corner pinnacles that preceded it. The pinnacles should surely be rebuilt one day. It is sad that the 1960s was such a destructive period for church architecture, albeit here on a relatively small scale.

LEFT: *The 12th-century rib-vaulted sanctuary contains Street's mid-19th-century furnishings and his redecoration of the vault.*

BELOW: *The lower part of the magnificent west front has much good chevron work.*

ALL SAINTS, HILLESDEN

BUCKINGHAMSHIRE

illesden is in a remote situation, just over 3 miles (4.8km) south of Buckingham. It is clear, however, that the magnificent early Tudor church that stands here was once directly connected to the great house and park that lay just over the wall to the east. In fact, there is even a bricked-up doorway from the upper floor of the north-east vestry that once led, via a bridge, to the house. In 1643, during the English Civil War, the house was besieged and then burnt by Parliamentary troops under the personal command of Oliver Cromwell. Another house was built on the site, but this was knocked down in the early 19th century, just after the young George Gilbert Scott saw it on a visit from his home at nearby Gawcott.

The parish church at Hillesden was described in 1493 as being in very poor condition, and one can see straight away that the entire building must have been completely rebuilt, with the exception of the western tower, soon after this. In the Middle Ages, the church was owned by Notley Abbey, which is believed to have paid for the rebuilding work. However, it is more

ABOVE: *The view east to the rood screen and beautiful chancel; the south transept, with its fine glass, is to the right.*

BELOW: *The enchanting early Tudor church as seen from the south, with its four large central windows of stained glass.*

133

probable that a wealthy family living in the parish paid for the rebuilding of the church and incorporated their own chantry chapel and its associated vestry at the same time. They may have started to build a new house immediately to the east at the same period, but nothing is documented until 1547, when the Denton family acquired the house and used the former chantry chapel as a family pew and burial place.

The church itself is now a beautiful late Perpendicular building with a nave, aisles, small transepts and a highly decorated chancel and north chapel with stone wall panelling. The porch also has panelled sides, with a fan-vault above it that was put in by George Gilbert Scott.

A row of beautifully carved angels can be seen high up on the north and south sides and, despite the battering the church had at Cromwell's hands, some fragments of the original stained glass can still be seen, particularly at the tops of the windows. The east window of the south transept has eight splendid scenes depicting the life of St Nicholas, and a new south window was added here by George Gilbert Scott in the 19th century.

This great Victorian architect was born at Gawcott, just 2 miles (3.2km) north of Hillesden. As a fifteen-year-old, he was entranced by the church and drew it. He said it was 'the first building which directed my attention to Gothic architecture'. At the end of his life he gave his services to the restoration of the church for free, paying for the fan-vault and the four pinnacles on top of the porch.

LEFT: *Scenes from the life of St Nicholas fill the east window of the south transept; this is a miraculous survival of early 16th-century stained glass.*

ST MARY, FELMERSHAM

BEDFORDSHIRE

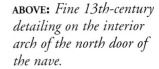

elmersham, which is situated a few miles north-west of Bedford on a rise above the Great Ouse, is a rarity – a major new church of the early part of the 13th century that is purely a parish church. In the late 12th century, it was given by Robert of Meppershall to Lenton Priory, a Cluniac house in Nottinghamshire, but why they chose to build a large new church here from about 1220 is unknown. This was a time when the new Gothic architecture was being enthusiastically taken up, and the largest of the new buildings was, of course, Salisbury Cathedral. There were also a handful of smaller, but architecturally grand buildings, for example Potterne or West Walton churches (see pages 58–9 and 161–2), built at the same time, Felmersham being one of the finest of these.

St Mary's has a four-bay aisled nave, with beautiful arcades and alternating round and octagonal shafts. The west front is particularly elegant, with a deeply moulded west portal, flanked by blind panels with plate tracery in the heads – the original windows were only lancets. Above this is a beautiful false gallery, which was unusable, with a row of seven arched openings and a mass of monolithic shafts. Higher still are the three large, shafted west windows, though the central one has Perpendicular tracery and a depressed head.

As was usual for the 13th century, the nave aisles originally had very low shed roofs – the lines of these are visible outside the west front – but these were raised and flattened and large windows were put in the outer walls in the 14th century. The north and south doorways date from the 13th century, and the doors themselves are also medieval. Internally, they, and the west doorway, have fine shouldered low-pitched two-centred arches over them, as can be seen in many of the buildings of Henry III's time, for example Westminster Abbey. There is also a fine sanctuary ring (not a knocker) on the south door.

The four crossing piers are equally fine examples of early Gothic mouldings, as is the tower above them – the crenellated top stage was added in the 15th century. To the east is a large chancel, although many of the lancets here were restored between 1853 and

ABOVE: *Fine 13th-century detailing on the interior arch of the north door of the nave.*

BELOW: *St Mary's has a large crossing tower and relatively small south transept.*

1854, when the large east window with reticulated tracery was also put in. North and south of the crossing, large transepts were planned, and the one on the north, which is now mostly filled with the organ, is of a reasonable size and has the tower stair-turret on the south-east. The south transept was clearly intended to be larger, but was never enlarged beyond the small-scale space that we can still see. The large flying buttresses on either side, to support the tower, indicate where the main walls were to have been when it was extended to the south.

In the late Middle Ages, the nave walls were raised for big clerestory windows and given crenellated parapets. The late-medieval nave roof was supported internally by posts on magnificent large carved corbels. There is also a fine rood screen at the entrance to the chancel, but, unfortunately, the loft above it was taken down during the 19th-century restoration.

RIGHT: *The view through the 15th-century rood screen, which still has its original colouring, to the chancel. The east window beyond dates from 1853.*

ST ETHELDREDA, HATFIELD

HERTFORDSHIRE

atfield is now most famous for the magnificent house that sits within a fine park, and which was built for Robert Cecil (1563–1612), 1st Earl of Salisbury, between 1608 and 1612. This house replaced an earlier brick palace, which was built at the end of the Middle Ages by the Lord Bishops of Ely. The work on the 'Old Palace', as it is now called, was started by Bishop John Morton in about 1480; however, he went on to be Archbishop of Canterbury in 1486 and the work was probably completed by his successor, John Alcock. The bishop's palace was used by Henry VIII from the 1520s; and from 1538 to 1607, Hatfield was a royal palace, with the king using it as a residence for his three children – later Edward VI, Mary I and Elizabeth I. Elizabeth actually learnt of her accession in 1558 at Hatfield.

ABOVE: *A detail of Victory in a 1920 window commemorating the three sons of the rector, Lord William Cecil, all of whom were killed in the First World War.*

BELOW: *The Brocket chantry chapel can be seen here in the foreground.*

OPPOSITE TOP: *Effigies of Elizabeth Moore (died 1612), second wife of Sir John Brocket, and her mother, Dame Agnes Saunders (died 1588).*

OPPOSITE BOTTOM: *This superb memorial is to Robert Cecil, 1st Earl of Salisbury (died 1612).*

BELOW: *The nave was rebuilt in 1872 for Lord Salisbury, the late 19th-century Prime Minister.*

Long before all this, King Edgar gave the manor of Hatfield to the Benedictine monks of Ely in about AD 970. After the Norman Conquest, Ely was rebuilt as a huge new monastery, and then in 1109 the abbot became the first Bishop of Ely, taking over the manor at Hatfield. It was now called Bishop's Hatfield, and by the late Middle Ages it was an important residence for the bishop on the route between Ely and London.

The dedication of the church to St Etheldreda – her popular name was St Audrey – who founded the monastery on the island of Ely in AD 673, still proclaims the Ely connection. It may have been in the late Saxon period that the first church was erected at Hatfield by monks. The earliest part of the present church, however, is the eastern arm, which dates from the 13th century. By this date it was already a large church, with transepts and unusual chapels to the west.

Unfortunately, the nave was completely rebuilt in 1872 and given a new raised roof. This was the great Victorian restoration that saw the

Perpendicular windows revert to Decorated ones, the box pews and three-decker pulpit removed and new pews and central heating put in.

In the 15th century, the fine west tower was built and a chantry chapel was made for the Brocket family on the south side of the chancel. It still contains some fine, but rather decayed tombs and monuments. Brocket Hall is 3 miles (4.8km) north of Hatfield, and in the early 19th century it was the home of Lord Melbourne (1779–1848), Queen Victoria's first Prime Minister and mentor. He was buried in the churchyard in 1848, alongside his even more famous, but somewhat tragic, wife, Lady Caroline Lamb (1785–1828).

On the north-east side of the church is the large family chapel for the Salisburys, which was built in 1618, soon after the completion of the new Hatfield House. It is a mortuary chapel – chantries had been abolished in 1548 – and at its centre is the very fine monument to Robert Cecil, who was Elizabeth I's Lord Treasurer, and was created the 1st Earl of Salisbury by James I

(1603–25). The monument shows the earl on a black marble slab, held up by the kneeling allegorical figures of Faith, Justice, Fortitude and Prudence. Below the slab is a macabre carving of the earl's skeleton on a plain straw mat. Nearby is a very different bronze effigy depicting the 3rd Marquis of Salisbury (1830–1903), another of Queen Victoria's famous Prime Ministers. This is a replica of Salisbury's monument in Westminster Abbey, and it was he who had the chapel elaborately refurnished in 1871 by Italian artisans. Particularly notable are the superb early 18th-century iron gates into the chapel, which came from Amiens Cathedral, and the Shap granite columns in the south arcade.

The church sits in its fine churchyard, which has magnificent ironwork gates from St Paul's Cathedral, just outside the old main gatehouse to Hatfield 'Old Palace', once the main way into the great house. It is now beside a peaceful cul-de-sac as a much grander new entrance to the house was constructed to the north.

THE EASTERN COUNTIES

This area is dominated by some of the largest and richest churches in Britain. In addition, Framlingham also contains some of the finest 16th-century monuments in England while Bradwell is a 7th-century church. The 12th-century wall paintings at Copford and Ickleton are rare survivals, and early 14th-century Cley has superb architecture and tracery. There are large town churches with long and complicated architectural histories, while West Walton, with its spectacular free-standing bell-tower is a major church of the early 13th century. This is just a small selection of twelve of the most interesting churches in a region of England that had about 1,500 churches in the late Middle Ages.

OPPOSITE: *Long Melford – one of the largest and most spectacular churches in England. To the right is the completely separate Lady chapel, which is an exceptional building in its own right.*

THE EASTERN COUNTIES

- Cley next the Sea
- Cromer
- North Walsham
- King's Lynn
- West Walton
- RUTLAND
- Wisbech
- NORFOLK
- Norwich
- Great Yarmouth
- Peterborough
- Lowestoft
- Corby
- CAMBRIDGESHIRE
- Ely
- Thetford
- Diss
- Blythburgh — Southwold
- Framlingham
- Cambridge
- SUFFOLK
- Bedford
- Lavenham
- Long Melford
- Ickleton
- Ipswich
- BEDFORDSHIRE
- Luton
- Stevenage
- Colchester
- Copford
- HERTFORDSHIRE
- ESSEX
- Clacton-on-Sea
- Harlow
- Bradwell-on-Sea
- Watford
- Brentwood
- GREATER LONDON
- Basildon
- Southend-on-Sea
- Slough
- LONDON

ST PETER, BRADWELL-ON-SEA

ESSEX

This very remote church is situated at the very end of a Roman road on raised ground above marshland, facing out to the sea. It is a very rare survival of a mid-7th century 'Kentish' type church, and similar churches in north-east Kent are almost all now ruined. Sadly, its closest parallel, which is situated at Reculver, directly across the Thames estuary from Bradwell, was a magnificent parish church until it was reduced to a ruin by the vicar in 1809. Only its twin western towers, which were purchased by Trinity House, the organization responsible for maintaining coastal landmarks, are intact and function as a seamark.

Both Bradwell and Reculver churches sit on the sites of late 3rd-century Roman 'Saxon shore' forts. The churches were constructed with reused Roman materials from the forts, both of which have been partially eroded by the sea. Bradwell church sits right across the line of its fort's west wall (the fort walls here were excavated in 1864 and 1947), and all that now remains is the very

tall rectangular nave, which had been reduced to a barn by the 17th century. Documentary evidence tells us that it still had a chancel and a west tower in the mid-15th century. The barn was restored and re-consecrated as a chapel by the Bishop of Chelmsford in 1920.

At first sight the surviving remains are rather dull with a modern altar on 20th-century paving in a plain rectangular structure. However, closer examination of the fabric reveals much of interest. On the west and north are broken-off remains of external buttresses. On the outside, to the east, the line of the original apse is marked out on the ground, and flanked by the plan of the walls of the north and south *porticus*. These little chambers were entered by doors from the church and the remains of their jambs can still be seen. In the east wall, quite high up, and visible inside and out, the remains of Roman brick arches can be viewed. Originally there was a triple opening into the apsidal sanctuary, with a pair of columns in the middle. An exact parallel to this survived at Reculver until 1809. The west doorway into the church is the original one and there is also an original window with a Roman brick arch above it. The scars for the west porch walls can also be seen. The windows in the side walls of the nave have also been opened up and partly restored.

Bede tells us that in AD 654 St Cedd came to Ythanceaster in Essex (almost certainly the Saxon name for the Roman fort of Othona) to help King Sigbert convert his people. The site of this church at Bradwell must be the place he came to set up his new monastery. He returned north for the Synod of Whitby (see pages 220–21) in AD 664 and died not long afterwards at his other monastery at Lastingham (see pages 218–19). The church that we still see was probably put up for him in the 650s, but the form of the building suggests that he had help from the monks across the Thames estuary in north-east Kent.

BELOW: *The original arches in the east wall of the nave have been filled in but are still visible.*

ST MICHAEL, COPFORD

ESSEX

This unusual church lies just 5 miles (8km) south-west of Colchester in a fairly remote situation. Immediately to its north, however, is Copford Hall, which belonged to the bishops of London throughout the Middle Ages, and it is likely that when the church was first built in about 1100, this was a private chapel for the bishop. The building had just a four-bay nave, with an eastern apsidal sanctuary, and, exceptionally, there was a masonry barrel-vault over the entire nave and chancel. Its nearest parallel is the chapel in the late 11th-century undercroft of the huge royal castle keep at nearby Colchester. St Michael's chapel, just like Colchester's keep, is built with much reused Roman material, which probably originated at a nearby villa. The Roman bricks in the

arches are particularly prominent. Inside, the whole building was plastered and, uniquely, quite large areas of early 12th-century wall paintings have survived, although these were very heavily restored and repainted in 1872 and 1880 and waxed between 1931–2. This means that, while we can now understand the paintings more easily, we have to accept that much of what can now be seen is Victorian. The nave vault, which was perhaps also covered in paintings, was destroyed in the late Middle Ages, but the semicircular vault over the sanctuary still survives. It features an image of Christ in Majesty, surrounded by angels with apostles below, and a zodiac cycle on the entrance arch. In the nave there is a well-preserved image depicting the Raising of Jairus's daughter on the north wall and fragments of other scenes.

In the late 12th century, an arch was broken through the south wall for a small chapel, and this was extended into a south aisle in the later 13th century. The central triple-chamfered archway into this aisle is made with new 13th-century bricks, a great rarity at this date. The scissor-braced roof over the church also perhaps dates from the late 13th century, although crown-posts were added in the 15th century. By the 13th century, the chapel had become a parish church, and a fine font, fashioned from Purbeck marble, was installed. The eastern bay of the nave was added to the sanctuary to form a chancel, and this was separated from the nave by a late medieval choir screen. One other remarkable survival is the original north door, which has fragments of skin on it. This is apparently human skin, rather than animal skin – and possibly belonged to a Viking invader! Conservation work on the wall paintings started in 1989, and has shed new light on them, revealing more about the patronage of an early 12th-century Bishop of London.

OPPOSITE, BELOW RIGHT: The springing points for an earlier barrel-vault are still present in the nave; the arch on the right is made with 13th-century bricks.

BELOW: Christ in Majesty is depicted on the apse vault in the sanctuary. This Romanesque painting was almost totally repainted by the Victorians.

HOLY TRINITY, LONG MELFORD

SUFFOLK

ABOVE: *Detail of the alabaster relief of Mary lying in after childbirth found outside the entrance to the Clopton chapel.*

One of the grandest parish churches ever built in England, this superb structure was created out of the huge profits of cloth-making, which flourished in this area of southern Suffolk. The county's other very large church is at Lavenham, just 4 miles (6.5km) to the north-east (see pages 148–9).

Including its separate Lady chapel at the eastern end, and its western tower, this church is almost 250 feet (75 metres) long – the size of a small cathedral. It is situated at the top end of a large, triangular-shaped village green, although the view of the church from the south was rather spoiled by the building of Trinity Hospital in 1573, which was enlarged in 1847.

By the later 14th century there was already a large church here, but all that remains of this church are the five western piers in the nave. The whole of the rest of the church was completely rebuilt in the half century after 1460, with the town's clothiers banding together to fund the work. We know many of their names because of the remarkable series of inscriptions on the walls that record this. By 1481 the amazing clerestory, with a row of eighteen windows on either side and a crenellated parapet, was under construction. A few years after this the two large chantry chapels at the

LEFT: *The outstanding east façade of the large Lady chapel; after the Reformation the building was used as a school.*

eastern end of the aisles were rebuilt for the two richest families, the Cloptons on the north and the Martyns on the south. A new projecting sanctuary was also installed, lit by very tall three-light windows.

The Cloptons lived at Kentwell Hall, three-quarters of a mile (1.2km) north of the church. When the rebuild of the main church was completed in the 1490s, John Clopton decided that he would go even further and have a completely separate Lady chapel constructed. This was built to the east of the church, with its north-west corner touching an extraordinary new private chantry beyond the east wall of the earlier Clopton chantry. Both structures are of exceptional architectural interest, with the Lady chapel being designed as a central space with a little surrounding cloister.

Externally, however, this is not apparent, and the whole building is covered with three parallel roofs. The new Clopton chantry was also very cleverly worked out. It is placed on the north side of the sanctuary with an arched opening in the wall to take John Clopton's own tomb – he died in 1497 – and to double as an Easter sepulchre. Entrance to the new chantry from the old is gained via a tiny vestibule, which has a miniature fan-vault over it and a fireplace in its north wall – Clopton even thought of his chantry priests, saying masses for his soul in the winter!

Unfortunately, the great western tower was struck by lighting in 1711 and rebuilt in brick. This situation was skilfully reversed between 1898 and 1903, when the fine architect G.F. Bodley re-cased the tower in stone and flint and added four new pinnacles.

ABOVE: *The very large nave has a beautiful clerestory and an angel roof.*

LEFT: *The Lily crucifixion in the east window of the Clopton chapel.*

147

ST PETER AND ST PAUL, LAVENHAM

SUFFOLK

ABOVE: *The Spring parclose of c. 1525 has early Renaissance detailing.*

BELOW: *Lavenham church, seen here at sunset, has a magnificent late 15th-century tower which completely overshadows the 14th-century spirelet.*

The great 'cloth' church at Lavenham is perhaps the finest church in Suffolk, though its neighbour at Long Melford (see pages 146–7) is a very strong competitor. Lavenham, unlike at Long Melford, still has its original great tower, which stretches 141 feet (42 metres) high, although it lacks the top pinnacles. Suffolk is a county without building stone, so it has to be imported from elsewhere, at great expense. Here we find that the whole of the nave is faced with stone that has been brought from Casterton quarry, just north of Stamford in Lincolnshire.

By the mid-15th century there must already have been a large church here, with aisles and eastern chantry chapels, but only the 14th-century chancel survives from this building with an eastern vestry added in 1444. The early 14th-century Decorated tracery in the east window and in one on the south-east, and the wide chancel arch, with a rare 14th-century screen beneath, are now the main features of this earlier building.

In 1485, the Battle of Bosworth resulted in the accession of a new king, Henry VII (1485–1509), who founded the Tudor dynasty. One of his greatest supporters was John de Vere (1433–1513), the 13th Earl of Oxford and owner of the manor of Lavenham. He joined with the very wealthy clothiers of the town, including Thomas Spring II, who was the richest of these, to instigate the total rebuilding of the church. In 1486, work first began on the great west tower, with its elegant buttresses and knapped flintwork. This was soon followed by the total rebuilding of the nave with its prodigal use of freestone, and its masses of large windows. At the south-east end of the nave, the 14th-century spirelet was left, slightly oddly, for the Sanctus bell. At the eastern ends of the aisles, two beautiful chantry chapels were built: the Holy Trinity chapel on the north for the Simons was followed in 1525 by the more elaborate Lady chapel on the south for the Springs.

Inside the building, the elaborately carved arcades and clerestories are very fine indeed, but the most exceptional features are the parclose screens at the east ends of the aisles. Both are supreme masterpieces of the woodcarvers' art. On the north is the Spring parclose, which is the more elaborate. It screened off an eastern altar, which was destroyed in 1548, and the tomb of the 'Rich Clothier' Thomas Spring III and his wife, Alice. This Thomas Spring, who died in 1523, asked for a parclose to be made round his tomb in front of St Katherine's altar. He also left money for 'the fynishing of the Stepul'. The other, less elaborate, parclose on the south now contains only a tomb that was put there in 1908. It was perhaps originally made for another clothier, Thomas Spourne.

The beautiful south side of the church is completed by a porch, in front of the main doorway (the north porch was never completed). It is the most obvious monument to the patronage of John de Vere. All the family arms are displayed above the doorway, while in the

ABOVE: *The 15th-century nave leads into the 14th-century chancel via the very rare survival of a 14th-century chancel screen. The Spring parclose is on the extreme left.*

spandrels are two Oxford boars. The figures of St Peter and St Paul were made by Eric Winters, and placed there in 1963.

ST MICHAEL, FRAMLINGHAM

SUFFOLK

ABOVE: *This fine organ case is part of the 1674 Thamar organ, which was brought here from Pembroke College, Cambridge in 1708.*

BELOW: *This detail of the magnificent tomb of Henry Howard, Earl of Surrey, shows one of his sons kneeling beside the tomb.*

ramlingham still contains one of the finest castles in England, featuring a magnificent high curtain wall and thirteen towers that were built at the very end of the 12th century by the Bigods, who were earls of Norfolk. To the south, just beyond the outer ditch, is the large parish church, which lies in the middle of this market town. Inside the church, the tall engaged piers on either side of the chancel arch and the carved capitals and bases also date from the late 12th century, indicating that there was already a large church here by this date.

The nave of the church was rebuilt in the 14th century, and the five bays of arcading, outer walls, Decorated tracery windows and a wall painting of the Holy Trinity all date from this period. In the late 15th century work started on the building of the tall flint-faced west tower, which rises nearly 100 feet (30 metres). Not long afterwards plans were put in hand to rebuild the nave clerestory, and after a change in design here – which is revealed by the redundant wall-shafts for roof trusses – a superb new clerestory and roof were built.

Externally, the clerestory windows are flanked by fine flushwork decoration, while inside one of the finest hammer-beam roofs in East Anglia can be seen. The hammer-beams themselves are concealed behind superb runs of timber fan-vaults on either side of the roof, which also frame the richly moulded clerestory windows. The work was perhaps finished in about 1520, when the eastern arches of the nave were rebuilt for a large rood screen that has since disappeared. The battlements on the tower were completed in 1534.

Most remarkable of all is the large chancel and its two vast chapels on either side, which incredibly were rebuilt in the reign of Edward VI (1547–53), at a time when such fittings were being destroyed.

The big bare east end of the church now contains one of the finest groups of early Renaissance tombs in England. To the north of the high altar is the tomb of Henry Fitzroy, Duke of Richmond, an illegitimate son of Henry VIII (1509–47) who was betrothed to Mary, the daughter of the 3rd Duke of Norfolk, Thomas Howard, (1473–1554). Fitzroy died in 1536, at the age of 16 and was buried at Thetford Priory. When this was dissolved in 1540, his remains were removed to Framlingham, and the fine tomb was not finished until 1555, just after the 3rd Duke's own death. The Duke's own tomb, to the south of the high altar, was completed in 1559, and it is one of the great master-pieces of early Renaissance art in England. The effigies of the Duke and Duchess lie on top of the tomb, which is surrounded by carved figures of the apostles, set in shell-headed recesses.

In the north-east corner of the church is the tomb of the two wives of the 4th Duke of Norfolk, Mary FitzAlan, who died in 1557, and Margaret Audley, who died in 1563. This superb tomb was once surmounted by a great canopy, but only the bases now remain.

To the west lies a totally different tomb, which was not made until 1614. Covered in coloured stones, painted and surrounded by the

kneeling figures of their sons and daughters, this is the tomb of the Earl and Countess of Surrey. The Earl was the son of the 3rd Duke of Norfolk and father of the 4th. In the last months of the reign of Henry VIII, Henry, who was known as the 'Poet Earl of Surrey', was arrested, along with his father. In January 1547, just before the king's death, Surrey was beheaded. Norfolk himself just escaped the block and died in his bed. In November 1547, the churchwardens sold their church plate 'to build up the church, the which my lord of Norfolk did pluck down to the intent to make it bigger.'

The final monument, in the south-east corner of the church, is much more modest. It is to Sir Robert Hitcham, who bought the manor of Framlingham from the Howards in 1635, and then gave the patronage of the church to Pembroke College, Cambridge after his death the following year. At the west end of the church is a very rare 17th-century organ, which was given to the church in 1708.

ABOVE: *The church's tower and clerestory date from the early 16th century.*

RIGHT: *On one panel of the font an angel is seen holding a shield with the symbol of the Holy Trinity, while on the stem are alternating lions and wild men.*

HOLY TRINITY, BLYTHBURGH

SUFFOLK

ABOVE: *A detail of the superb painted angel roof.*

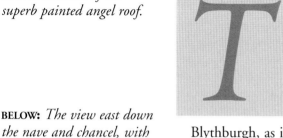

BELOW: *The view east down the nave and chancel, with their very long clerestory and roof.*

T his is one of the most magnificent churches in coastal Suffolk, but it is also flawed because many of its original interior fittings have been stripped out. Despite this, the huge 128-foot (38-metre) long church, which dominates the marshland that surrounds it, is a magnificent work of architecture, dating largely from the mid-15th century. Its most prominent feature, a tall and rather plain west tower that once had a spire, is the only vestige of an earlier 14th-century church. It is likely that this was supposed to have been rebuilt with the rest of the church, but funds probably ran out.

Blythburgh, as its name suggests, was a very important ramparted town (a burgh) of the late Anglo-Saxon period. It was probably a 7th-century royal and Christian settlement that had to be fortified during the period of Viking raids. In the later medieval period it was an important

market town and port beside a fine natural haven on the River Blyth. The haven was nearly closed off from the sea on the north and south by the shingle spits near the later settlements of Walberswick to the south and Southwold to the north. All three towns became very wealthy from their port incomes in the later 15th century and constructed fine churches. Blythburgh reverted to being a small village in the post-medieval period, and today it suffers greatly from the busy A12, which cuts the old town in half.

The most spectacular view of the church is that from the south where the external decoration is the most elaborate. This side also has a magnificent porch in front of the principal doorway into the church, and it is clear that this was the way the church was intended to be seen by travellers coming up the main road from Ipswich. The northern side of the church is almost as grand, and this was seen by ships in the haven.

The exterior of the church is covered by vast areas of traceried windows and flintwork. On the buttresses are fine areas of 'flushwork' – beautiful inlaid areas of a knapped tabular flintwork – which are set into the masonry panels. Under the great east window is a flushwork inscription in Lombardic letters, and there is more flushwork decoration on either side of the east window.

As one enters the two-storey stone vaulted porch, it becomes clear that the whole outer face is covered in tabular flint with a large statue niche in the centre. This now contains a slightly strange modern statue of the Holy Trinity.

Inside the church the first impression is of brick paving, clear tracery windows and white-wash. However, beautiful stone arcades can also be seen, and above the central part of the nave much survives of a wonderful painted angel roof. Despite the later stripping out, enough remains of the pre-Reformation features to provide a good idea of the form of the late medieval church. In the centre of the western end is a fine, although partly mutilated, carved font. This stands in its original position on a two-stepped octagonal base in the walking passage between the north and south doorways. The original doors also survive with tracery on their exteriors. At the eastern end of the church the chancel is still marked by a wooden screen, although the upper part is modern. The screens to the north and south are more complete, but they also lack their lofts, which were small galleries above the screens that were reached from a masonry stair in a wider buttress outside the north wall of the church. East of the aisle screens were chantry chapels with their own separate doors, which were set beneath pierced buttresses. The chapel on the north contained the chantry for the family of John Hopton, who died in 1478, and between the chantry and the sanctuary is a beautiful, carved Purbeck marble tomb set into the wall, which also doubled as the Easter sepulchre. The tomb-chest once

displayed the brasses of John Hopton and his two wives – Margaret, who died in 1452, and Thomasine, who died in 1497 – although only the indents now survive. Hopton was Lord of Blythburgh manor and one of the wealthy men who paid for the rebuilding of the church.

Today the church is often used as a small concert hall for the Aldeburgh Festival, with the core of the audience still sitting on low medieval benches that have fine carved figures of the seasons and seven deadly sins on the ends.

ABOVE: *Carved figures of St Matthias and St Bartholomew decorate the stall fronts, and may once have been part of the rood screen.*

BELOW: *The church stands on the former haven of the River Blyth.*

ST EDMUND, KING AND MARTYR, SOUTHWOLD

SUFFOLK

ABOVE: *A late medieval bench-end vividly portrays someone pulling an obscene face.*

During the early Norman period, Southwold, sitting on its island at the mouth of the River Blyth, barely existed. The area's main village and parish church were at Reydon, 1½ miles (2.4km) to the north-west. Later Southwold, with its natural harbour, started to become an important settlement. In 1202, John de Grey, the Bishop of Norwich, instructed that a chapel at the very least should be built here. The manor was owned by the abbot and monks of the great Benedictine abbey at Bury, where the relics of St Edmund (841–69), the martyred Anglo-Saxon king of East Anglia, were enshrined. This is why Southwold's chapel, which became the parish church, was dedicated to the saint. In the later Middle Ages much coastal erosion took place to the south of the Blyth, eventually destroying the important town of Dunwich nearby, which Southwold profited from.

The 13th-century church was probably destroyed in a fire, but there is no doubt that the present large church was built in a continuous campaign between the 1430s and the end of the century. Many of the wealthy townspeople gave money for the work – there is surviving documentation for this in their wills – and the abbey at Bury probably paid in part for the relatively small chancel. The church is a large, continuously aisled, structure that is 160 feet (48 metres) long, with a magnificent

RIGHT: *The church is exceptional for the superb painted panelling on the lower part of the rood screen, with beautifully drawn figures of the apostles; this dates from the late 15th century.*

OPPOSITE: *The superb flint and flushwork exterior is a mixture of 15th- and 19th-century facings.*

154

ABOVE: *The figure known as Southwold Jack probably originates from a 15th-century clock.*

LEFT: *The high angel roof of the chancel was restored and redecorated in 1857.*

western tower 100 feet (30 metres) high. Externally it is almost entirely covered with very hard, knapped flint with dressings of magnesian limestone from South Yorkshire and Caen stone. The flint was used most effectively as flushwork – squared, knapped flint used with dressed stone for decoration. This is most obvious in the plinth all the way round and in the checker patterns on the sides of the porch. Over the west window, in flushwork, is written SCT. EDMUND ORA P. NOBIS ('Pray for us St Edmund'). Much of the rest of the flintwork is a 19th-century restoration, and the copper roof is very unmedieval!

Inside, the wonderful choir stalls, which are return stalls with seven seats on either side, may have come from elsewhere shortly after the Reformation. There are many other fine fittings, including the slender pulpit, which was over-restored and gilded in 1928, the font and a very rare circular Elizabethan communion table. There is also a piscina with niches above and sedilia south of the high altar, all with coved-out panelled ceilings. The high altar itself is now surmounted by F.E. Howard's richly gilded reredos of 1929, and above this, the east window is filled with Sir Ninian Comper's stained glass.

ST MARGARET, CLEY NEXT THE SEA

NORFOLK

Norfolk contains a huge number of medieval churches, and on the county's north coast there are great concentrations of them around places such as Burnham. Cley's church, which was originally coastal and is now inland, once looked south (the town itself migrated north in the 17th century) over its market and haven on the River Glaven. It is an exceptional building, largely dating from the early 14th century, but also with some fine later 15th-century work.

ABOVE: *A detail of the sacrament of Baptism on the font.*

The oldest surviving work is the lower part of the north-west tower. This indicates a date in the 13th century, and the weather-mould on its east side suggests that the earliest nave was immediately east of this. By the early 14th century, the town of Cley was flourishing, and the bold decision was taken to demolish the whole church, apart from the

BELOW: *The church has an unroofed south transept, which is now walled off from within, and a fine 15th-century south porch.*

LEFT: *Nave corbel-stops depict everything from St George and the Dragon to a musician and a lewd imp.*

ABOVE: *The remarkable early 14th-century nave has a unique clerestory with circular windows through which light pours in.*

north-west tower and the chancel. The intention was to build a very large new aisled nave with eastern transept-chapels. This new nave is justly famous for its fine six-bay arcades surmounted by its amazing clerestories of circular windows, filled with cusped cinquefoils. Between each circular window, more light is brought in through smaller two-light windows, which can be seen inside above a row of very fine statue niches. Each has a beautifully carved bracket with a tabernacle above. The hood-mould stops also have finely carved figures on them. Above the chancel arch was another window that is now filled in, and to the left and right were transept-chapels of equal distinction, which are both now ruined shells, as they were abandoned in the 17th century. The tracery of the great south window is particularly fine. On the south and west, both now enclosed in later porches, are the magnificent early 14th-century doorways. The west doorway still retains its original doors, which are covered with beautiful decorative ironwork hinges.

Despite the onset of the Black Death in the 14th century, Cley still flourished in the 15th century. The outer walls of the aisles were rebuilt and raised, and given new Perpendicular windows. Impressive new east and west windows were also installed, but the most splendid feature of this period is the great two-storey south porch, which has a tierceron vault inside. It also has beautiful filigree battlements and niches for statues in the buttresses. The shields on the entrance jambs commemorate the many prominent families who paid for all this work. Inside the church some of the late medieval fixtures remain, for example the font, which has the seven sacraments carved on its bowl, and the poppy-head bench ends.

After the Reformation, the story of Cley's church becomes less exciting. The transepts were walled off after the roofs were removed. In the last century or so, the building has undergone some restoration, and in 1973 the nave was completely re-roofed, and the masonry conserved.

ST MARGARET, KING'S LYNN

NORFOLK

The large parish for the southern part of Bishop's Lynn, as the town was called before 1536, suffered its greatest disaster at noon on 8 September 1741. A great storm blew down the upper part of the north-west tower, and its very splendid timber and lead spire, which was 258 feet (77.5 metres) high. It fell onto the nave and aisles and damaged the beautiful octagonal lantern tower, which was also constructed of timber and lead and resembled a smaller version of the octagon at Ely Cathedral. The rebuilding that followed was in a debased Perpendicular style and was completed by 1745, but alas, all the nave arcades and aisle walls were completely removed, as were the large transepts and the choir aisles and chapels. Only the core of the east and west ends were left.

Like Boston in Lincolnshire, Lynn probably started as a trading port on the edge of the Wash at the mouth of the River Nar in the late Anglo-Saxon period. Bishop Herbert de Losinga of Norwich developed the town from around 1100. The priory was a cell of the large new Benedictine priory at Norwich Cathedral, and it had its cloister and priory buildings to the south of the church.

The lowest part of the western towers of this new church still survives and is best seen on the south-west tower. Immediately to the west of this, facing onto the river front, was the bishop's Saturday market. The town expanded rapidly, particularly on its north side, in the 12th and 13th centuries, and two new churches were built. The town's trade increased further when the mouth of the Great Ouse migrated to Lynn from Wisbech in the late 13th century.

In the mid-13th century, the nave, crossing and choir were completely rebuilt at St Margaret's, but only the fine choir arcades with foliated capitals and much sculpture now show this. The column bases for the nave arcades can still be seen below the arcades that were built in 1745.

ABOVE: *A so-called 'Green Man' among the foliage of a misericord on the south side of the choir.*

BELOW: *The 13th-century chancel, with Bodley's great reredos of 1899.*

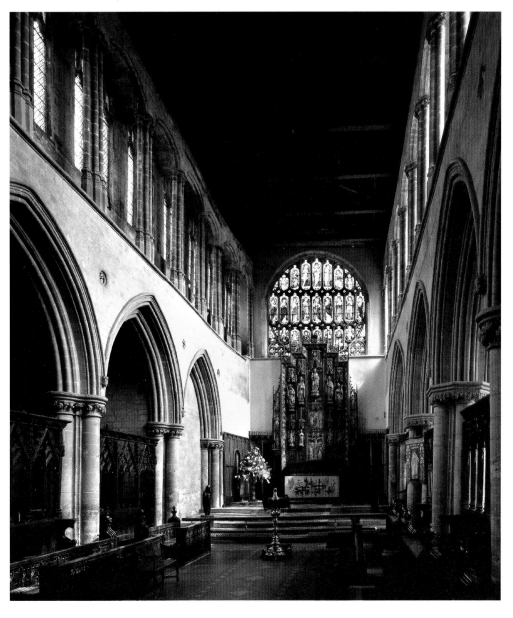

Other late medieval work was also done, but much of this was later destroyed. Important fragments do, however, remain, including the western bay of the outer north aisle, which is now a rather strange porch, and the extreme east end of the church, with its semi-octagonal turrets.

Inside, the church is a hotch-potch of relocated furnishings, some of which are excellent. In the south choir aisle are the large Flemish brasses of Adam Walsoken, who died in 1349, and Robert Braunche, who died in 1364, with the latter showing the peacock feast that was given to Edward III. There are also some very fine screen fragments and stalls with wonderful misericords. On the north side is a fine Snetzler organ, which dates from 1754, while at the east end of the building a fine reredos by G.F. Bodley was installed behind the high altar in 1899.

ABOVE: *The west front dates from several periods, but is no less impressive for it. The left-hand tower would have once carried a huge timber and lead spire.*

LEFT: *Details of two splendidly carved misericords in the choir stalls.*

ST MARY, WEST WALTON

NORFOLK

his is the most westerly church in Norfolk, as well as being one of the finest early 13th-century parish churches in England. When it was built, in about the 1230s, it was situated less than half a mile (0.8km) east of the large sea bank that bounded the estuaries of the Rivers Nene and Great Ouse. Storms, silt and the rising sea-level caused the mouth of the river to migrate eastwards to Kings Lynn from the later 13th century, but by this time the parish had a very large population that was still increasing. This was because large areas of the fens (the hitherto uninhabited marshes) to the south-east were being reclaimed, drained, populated and turned into arable and grazing land. Hence the very large floor area of the church itself.

The nave consists of six bays and had wide aisles on either side from the very first. It also had a large chancel that was flanked by chapels entered through pairs of arches on either side, although these are now blocked up. Unfortunately, the eastern end of the chancel was shortened by 4 feet (1.2 metres) in 1807 and rebuilt with a rather dull new east window.

The architecture of the church is quite exceptional, and can best be compared with the great

ABOVE: *The painted roundels in the spandrels above the nave arcade represent the twelve tribes of Israel. This one, on the north side, shows 'Naphtali, a hind let loose: he giveth goodly words'.*

BELOW: *St Mary's has a very large nave and a monumental south porch. The shadow in the foreground of this picture is produced by the huge bell-tower to the south.*

cathedrals of Lincoln and Ely to the north and south. The nave arcades have beautiful circular piers, each surrounded with four detached shafts of Alwalton marble, some of which have been restored with Purbeck marble. Alwalton is a local marble that was brought along the River Nene from just to the west of Peterborough. Above the piers are delicately carved stiff-leaf capitals, with heavily moulded arches above them. Above all of this is a magnificent continuous clerestory with windows in every second bay inside and third bay outside. The clerestory also had marble shafts all the way along, both inside and outside, although the latter were later removed. There is also a magnificent western doorway and an even more splendid south door and porch.

However, it is very clear that in the late Middle Ages the upper

elements of the church were damaged, and had to be rebuilt with new, shallow-pitched roofs and aisle windows. One original and superbly decorated window does survive on the south-east. The reason for this is almost certainly because of storm and subsidence damage as large buttresses have been added and the flanking chancel-chapels have been removed.

The other magnificent feature of this church is the very large, free-standing, 13th-century bell-tower to the south of the church. It now has a late medieval parapet and pinnacles, but may originally have had a spire. Remarkably, several other churches around the old Nene estuary, including those at Long Sutton, Tydd St Giles, Terrington St Clement and Terrington St John, also had large free-standing bell-towers.

ST PETER AND ST PAUL, WISBECH

CAMBRIDGESHIRE

 n the Middle Ages Wisbech was at the head of the most important estuary on the Wash, with the River Nene and River Ouse flowing past it. From the late 13th century, however, the estuary at King's Lynn gradually rose to take prominence in the region. Soon after the Norman Conquest, a royal castle was built at Wisbech, which lay immediately west of the church. From the 12th century onwards the castle was held by the Bishop of Ely, and in about 1480 Bishop Morton, who was also Lord Chancellor and later Archbishop of Canterbury, rebuilt it as a new residence. Morton was also responsible for making the cut from Peterborough to Wisbech – called 'Morton's Leam' – which increased the flow of the River Nene and helped to keep the port open.

It is against this background that the remarkable church at Wisbech should be observed. The church has a highly unusual 'double' nave with a tall central arcade. Inside the church it is clear that it has a complicated architectural history, and that the northern nave was the earlier and more important structure. Its fine mid-12th-century north arcade still survives, and evidence discovered below ground during the Victorian restoration of George Gilbert Scott shows that there was a similar arcade on the south, along with a large west tower, the lower part of which still survives. All of this indicates that a large church stood on this site before 1200.

ABOVE: *The huge carved royal arms of James I now hang within an arch of the south nave arcade. By law, royal arms had to be erected in churches from the 16th century.*

BELOW: *Wisbech's spacious 'double' nave and off-centred chancel reflect the complex development of this church between the 12th and 15th centuries.*

ABOVE: *The east end of the church, with the large campanile to the right and the low Holy Trinity guild chantry on the left.*

A century after this, when the medieval population of Wisbech reached its peak, the church was enlarged again and given its present plan, with a second, outer south aisle, an enlarged north aisle and a greatly extended chancel and south chapel. The fine surviving arcades between the two south aisles and between the chancel and south chapel date from the late 13th century, as does the beautiful Decorated tracery window of the main south aisle. Most of the other windows were enlarged as the church was rebuilt in the 15th century, when a two-storey south porch was also added.

Sometime in the middle of the 15th century, the western tower collapsed eastwards onto the nave and south aisle, and it was after this that the church got its unique form with a new slender arcade placed down the centre and high clerestory windows above the north and south arcades. A new pitched roof was created over the double nave, with two flat ceilings on the inside. Early in the 16th century a small chapel, which is now the vestry, was added on the south-east for the Guild of the Holy Trinity. It has an elaborately decorated battlemented parapet.

The final addition to the church was the magnificent bell-tower, which also acts as the north porch. This is a free-standing structure, with its southern buttresses just touching the north aisle. It is the last of a series of free-standing bell-towers to be built in the unstable fenland region around the mouth of the River Nene.

RIGHT: *This fine monument is dedicated to Mathias Taylor and his wife; he died in 1633.*

ST MARY, ICKLETON

CAMBRIDGESHIRE

 ckleton now lies between two branches of the M11, 10 miles (16km) south of Cambridge, and only yards from the Essex border. At the time of Domesday Book, the manor belonged to Count Eustace of Boulogne, and there was a major settlement here as the mills, arable land and all the livestock are also carefully listed in Domesday Book. It was at this time that a very substantial aisled church was built here, probably paid for by Eustace. Remarkably, the west doorway, nave arcades and the base of the crossing tower still survive from this late 11th-century church. The wonderful flat Barnack stone cushion capitals, which are similar to those in the late 11th-century crypt at Rochester Cathedral, sit on mainly monolithic shafts. Very plain semi-circular arches,

ABOVE: *St Michael weighing the souls of the dead adorns a bench-end.*

BELOW: *The late 11th-century nave looks east to the 13th-century crossing and the Doom painting high on the east wall.*

ABOVE: *The top section of the 14th-century Doom painting shows Christ in Judgement on a rainbow; this can be compared with that at St Thomas's, Salisbury (page 55). The Virgin on the left has bare breasts – a sign of supplication.*

BELOW: *The 12th-century underpainting depicts the Betrayal and Flagellation of Christ, and can be found on the north side of the nave.*

surmounted by the original single-splayed clerestory windows, are still intact on both sides from the west wall to the chancel arch. The large columns are said to be reused Roman ones, but this is unlikely.

On the evening of 24 August 1979, disaster struck when an arsonist set the church on fire, and much of the roofing was burnt. However, when the repairs were carried out an amazing discovery was made – many fresco wall paintings above the north arcade still existed. The scenes were probably painted in the later 12th century, soon after the parish church was given to the newly founded Benedictine nunnery of Ickleton, which lay just to the west of the church. What we see now are the remains of the underpainting of two tiers of scenes. The upper tier, which survives for two full bays, between the clerestory windows, shows four passion scenes – The Last Supper, Betrayal, Flagellation and Christ carrying the Cross. The lower tier, in the spandrels of the arches, shows three scenes of martyrdom – St Peter, St Andrew and St Laurence – and there are even surviving figures of apostles on the clerestory windows and window splays.

The north transept and chancel were demolished and rebuilt in the late 18th and 19th centuries, but the fine very wide early 14th-century south aisle still survives, with a large arch into the south transept chapel at its east end. There is a contemporary south porch, which was given a stone vault in the later 14th century. The upper part of the crossing tower (including the crossing arches) was rebuilt in the later 13th century, and on top of it is a fine timber and lead-covered spire. This was restored between 1991 and 1992, but it still contains many late 13th-century lap-jointed timbers, and projecting from its side is a late medieval Sanctus bell, which is now the clock bell.

Above the tall chancel arch, the upper part of a 14th-century Doom painting was also discovered after the 1979 fire. This is another remarkable survival, although sadly the lower section is no longer there. In the centre is Christ the Judge, with the Virgin Mary and St John on either side, as usual. However, the Virgin is shown with bare breasts, a gesture of supplication. At the entrance to the chancel is a narrow but tall painted rood screen.

OPPOSITE: *The church has a 13th-century tower and lead-covered spire with a unique Sanctus bell that projects from its south side.*

THE CENTRAL COUNTIES

This is a region dominated by beautiful spires, such as those found at Newark-on-Trent, Grantham, Louth and Brant Broughton, all influenced by the mother church at Lincoln. Central England is also graced with the huge church at Boston, with its towering 'stump'. By contrast, there is the exceptional collection of Anglo-Saxon sculptures at Breedon; the magnificent Romanesque bishop's church at Stow; and the large-aisled Romanesque basilica at Northampton. Not far away is the well-preserved Anglo-Saxon church at Brixworth, which also has a later spire. To the east of Brixworth is the very fine double church and spire at Higham Ferrers. Finally, Melton Mowbray's impressive church has its amazing clerestory with 144 windows.

OPPOSITE: *The vast aisled nave and chancel of Boston parish church have high, colourful roofs that were completely rebuilt by Sir Charles Nicholson in 1929–33.*

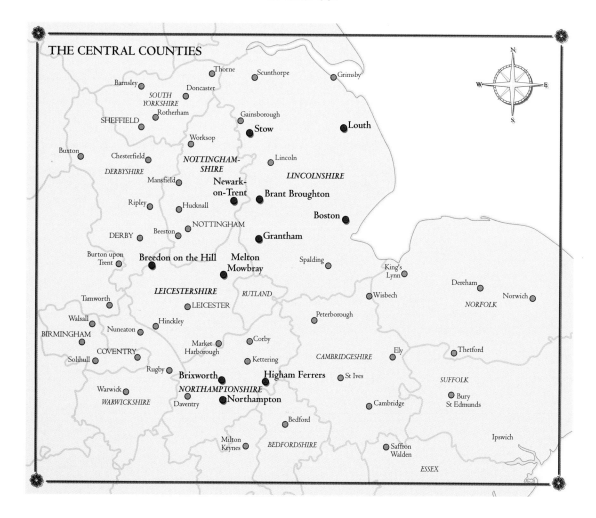

THE CENTRAL COUNTIES

ST PETER, NORTHAMPTON

NORTHAMPTONSHIRE

ABOVE: *The 12th-century south arcade butts up to the rebuilt south side of the tower arch.*

BELOW: *The early 17th-century west tower is full of reused 12th-century material.*

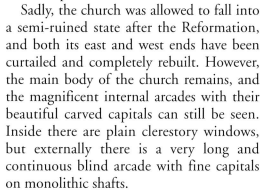

This fine large church, which lies to the west of the town centre in an area of modern dereliction, was once at the very centre of Anglo-Saxon and Norman Northampton. Immediately to the north-west, where the railway station now lies, was a great royal castle, most famous as the scene of a momentous confrontation between Henry II (1154–89) and his Archbishop of Canterbury, Thomas Becket, in October 1164, after which Becket fled into exile. This magnificent church must have been built a decade or so before this altercation, and hence Becket would have seen it newly completed with all its wonderful Romanesque sculptural decoration. There can be little doubt that the patron was either the king himself or Simon de Senlis, the 2nd Earl of Northampton.

Sadly, the church was allowed to fall into a semi-ruined state after the Reformation, and both its east and west ends have been curtailed and completely rebuilt. However, the main body of the church remains, and the magnificent internal arcades with their beautiful carved capitals can still be seen. Inside there are plain clerestory windows, but externally there is a very long and continuous blind arcade with fine capitals on monolithic shafts.

Very unusually for the Norman period, the nave runs directly into the chancel without a chancel arch, and it is only at the west end that there is a large tower arch. The original tower was reported to be in ruins in 1607 and some twenty years later it was dismantled. A completely new tower was built one bay to the east and this survives, but much of the 12th-century masonry was reused in it, including the tower arch, several lengths of the blind arcades (on the north, south and west external walls) and, most peculiarly, the earlier pillars, which acted as buttresses to the north-west and south-west angles of the tower. The tower also has a striped effect on its lower half and the presumed west doorway arch is set above the west window, without side jambs.

By the end of the Middle Ages, the eastern end of the church was squared off and probably rebuilt. This was in poor condition by the mid-19th century. George Gilbert Scott was brought in to restore the whole church in 1850, and he completely rebuilt and extended the eastern end, partially utilizing the old 12th-century foundations. For the new east wall he copied the east elevation of the chapel of the Hospital of St Cross at Winchester.

Archaeological excavations took place immediately to the east of the church in 1981–2 and uncovered the remains of an Anglo-Saxon palace complex, which included a great timber hall that was rebuilt in stone, probably in the 8th century. The excavations also uncovered the stone east wall of a major Anglo-Saxon church, which largely underlies the present building, thus confirming that there was a major place of worship here long before the Norman period.

BELOW: *The chancel has a new east wall, built by George Gilbert Scott, on either side of which are 12th-century arcades with highly decorated pier capitals.*

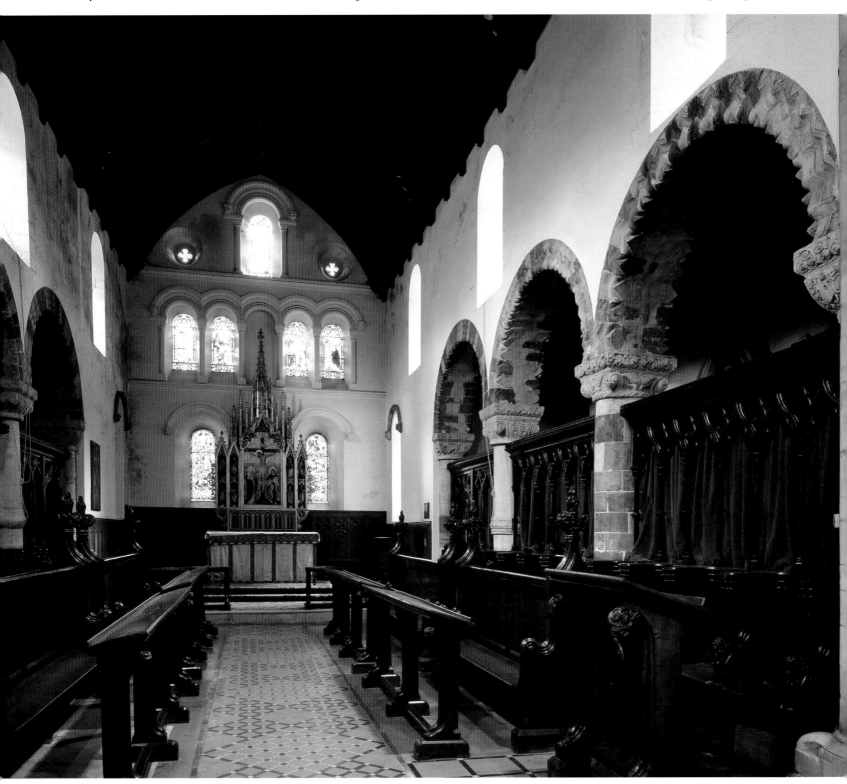

ALL SAINTS, BRIXWORTH
NORTHAMPTONSHIRE

Brixworth's church is probably the best-preserved Anglo-Saxon church to survive in England. A 12th-century source tells us that a monastery was founded here by Cuthbald, Abbot of Peterborough, in AD 675. The present structure was, however, probably built in the later Anglo-Saxon period, perhaps in the 9th or 10th century. Amazingly, the whole of the nave and chancel of the Anglo-Saxon building survive, though, as can be seen from the four blocked-up arches on either side, the lateral chambers or *porticus* were removed on both sides, probably in the 11th century.

The triple archway between the original nave and chancel was also cut away in the 14th century and replaced by a wide chancel arch, but the end of the Roman brick arches on either side can still be seen. Beyond this, the original archway into the apsidal sanctuary survives, flanked by two windows in the upper wall. The apse itself was rebuilt in the 19th century. Below it, however, and only visible on the exterior, was a 'ring crypt' – a barrel-vaulted passageway that ran all the way round the outside of the apse. The top of the outer wall of the ring crypt is no longer there, but its inner wall and the springing for the barrel-vault can still be seen. The ring crypt was originally entered from doorways at either end. These are still visible, but blocked-up, in the east wall of the chancel. At the far eastern end of the ring crypt, a short passage may have led back to an underground shrine in the centre, beneath the sanctuary, as happened most famously at St Peter's Church in Rome and in Anglo-Saxon Canterbury Cathedral.

At the western end of the present church is the tower and spire. The lowest section of this is also part of the original building, and acted as the west porch and original main doorway into the church. It, too, was flanked by *porticus* on either side, which perhaps formed the narthex to the

church. In the 11th century, after all the *porticus* had been removed, the west porch became a tower, with a large new spiral staircase on the west. A new doorway was created on the south side at the western end of the nave; this is still the main entrance, and its early Norman masonry is apparent. The eastern apsidal sanctuary was also rebuilt at this time, but it was given a square eastern end in the 15th century and restored as

an apse only in the 19th century, after the form of the Anglo-Saxon church was rediscovered.

On the south side of the chancel is a 13th-century Lady chapel, also called the Verdun chapel after Sir John de Verdun, whose fine tomb is there; he or his son probably built the chapel. The top of the tower, the fine stone spire and probably the crenellated nave and chancel parapets were all built in the early 14th century.

OPPOSITE: *The eagle of St John, just inside the south door, was possibly taken from an Anglo-Saxon cross.*

BELOW: *The wide 14th-century chancel arch replaced a triple arcade.*

ST MARY, HIGHAM FERRERS

NORTHAMPTONSHIRE

ABOVE: *This tomb was probably made for Henry, 3rd Earl of Lancaster, but never used by him.*

BELOW: *Comper's restored rood and rood loft create a fabulous centrepiece to the nave.*

igham, a small medieval town in eastern Northamptonshire, takes the second part of its name from the Ferrers family, who held the earldom of Derby and had a castle here, just to the north of the church. In the 13th century, the church underwent a programme of reconstruction, which was initially sponsored by the Ferrers. The chancel was rebuilt, followed by the new aisled nave, which had a magnificent west tower added to it in the mid-13th century. Higham was taken from the Ferrers family in 1266 and granted to Edmund Crouchback, Earl of Lancaster (1245–96), the second son of Henry III. During this period of change, the rebuilding work continued on a magnificent scale. The beautiful west tower, with its sculpted double west doorway and large tympanum, is of particular interest because of its resemblance to Henry III's reconstruction

of Westminster Abbey. Work on the tower was probably only completed after the change of ownership in 1266 and several changes of plan can be observed. The tower's architectural history is complicated by the collapse and rebuilding of the spire and upper part of the tower between 1631 and 1632.

The top of the tower, with its open-work frieze, and the spire itself were probably originally built early in the 14th century, although the principal work at this time was to double the size of the church with the construction of a northern nave with its own north aisle. To the east of this a fine new Lady chapel was built, which is as large as the earlier chancel to the south. Between the Lady chapel and chancel a large monumental tomb was prepared, which must have been for Henry, the 3rd Earl of Lancaster (1281–1345), who held the manor from 1327 until his death. In the event, he was buried at his new foundation in Leicester rather than here, and the brass of a rector, Laurence of St Maur, who died in 1338, was eventually placed on top of the tomb in 1633. This wonderful brass is one of the best in England, and it was probably originally set in the floor of the Lady chapel. This chapel also contains brasses of Archbishop Henry Chichele's parents and his brother and his wife. Chichele (1362–1443) was born in Higham Ferrers and was Archbishop of Canterbury from 1414 under Henry V (1413–22) and Henry VI. He founded a new college in his native town, which lay a little to the north-west of the church but is sadly now in ruins. He also founded the very famous All Souls' College at Oxford.

Around the church two of the archbishop's other institutions can also be seen: his school to the west, with a churchyard cross beside it, and his bedehouse (almshouse) to the south. Chichele also paid for the installation of clerestories and the raised low-pitched roofs in the church; and the chancel still contains twenty fine stalls replete with misericords for the members of his college. By the time of Chichele's death, the college had eight priests, including a master, grammar-master and song-master, as well as four clerks and six choristers. Sadly, the college was surrendered to Henry VIII in 1542 and abolished.

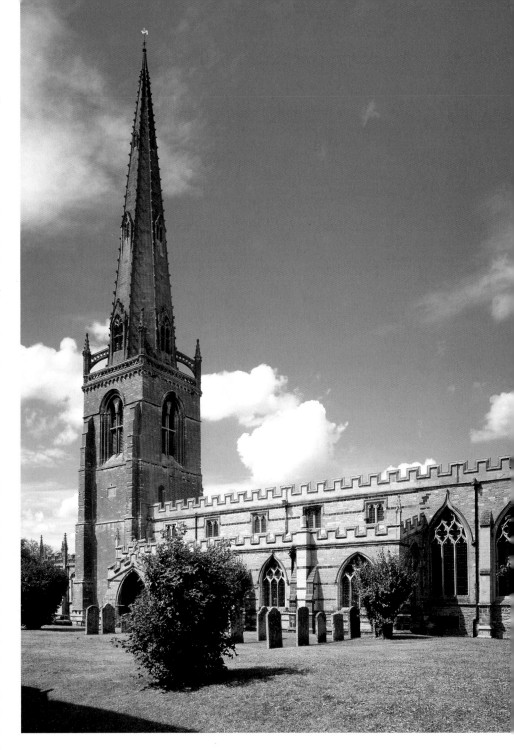

ABOVE: *The delicate 12th- and early 14th-century spire make St Mary's a majestic building.*

BELOW: *This misericord is one of twenty fine, carved tip-up seats provided by Archbishop Chichele.*

ST MARY AND ST HARDULPH, BREEDON ON THE HILL

LEICESTERSHIRE

ABOVE: *A figure carved in about* AD *800 holds a book and gives a blessing; it can now be found at the east end of the south aisle and is one of several similar early sculptures at this church.*

BELOW: *From the north-east, the larger nave would once have been to the right of the tower.*

I n north-west Leicestershire, very close to the border with Derbyshire, is a remarkable church that sits on top of a hard Carboniferous Limestone hill. More than half the hill has been quarried away, but in the late prehistoric period it was capped by a large hill fort, the bank, ditch and entrance to which are still visible on the western side of the site. Before the 7th century came to a close, a monastery was established inside the fort, which was attached to a larger monastery at Peterborough, some 50 miles (80km) to the east. Nothing of the Anglo-Saxon buildings of the monastery is now visible, but inside the present church, and reset in the walls, is one of the finest collections of Anglo-Saxon architectural sculpture in England. A series of frieze panels, including vine scroll, carved figures and birds, can be seen, as can fragments of larger blocks from cross-shafts and other large structures. The finest of all the remains, although it is sadly not easily visible as it is in the bell-ringing chamber, is the so-called 'Breedon Angel', one of the best Anglo-Saxon sculptures in the country (see page 9). Most of the sculpture probably dates from the late 8th to early 9th centuries and we know the monastery must have been devastated between AD 873 and 874, when the Vikings win-

tered at nearby Repton (see pages 200–201) – the Norsemen may also have used fortified Breedon as a base. Some of the church's sculpture may date from the late 10th century, when the monastery was revived.

After the Norman Conquest, a small Augustinian priory was created here, and this survived until the Dissolution in the 16th century. The lower part of the present west tower dates from the 12th century and was no doubt part of the early Augustinian buildings. To the east of this, a fine new aisled chancel was added in the 13th century. Exceptionally, the aisles had rib-vaults over them, though only the north aisle vault survives. West of the tower was probably the original nave and, before this, the Anglo-Saxon church, but this was abandoned after the Dissolution. Scars on the west wall of the tower and the south porch do, however, suggest that the nave was expanded southwards to form an aisled nave in the late Middle Ages.

With the monastery gone, a rich local man, Francis Shirley of Staunton, bought the priory church from Henry VIII and established his family pew and burial place in the chancel's north aisle. The parishioners of Breedon were then able to use the rest of the chancel as their church. Another remarkable survival in the church is the elaborate Shirley family pew to the west of the aisle. It dates from 1627 and has a vestibule and inner room surmounted by obelisks and shields of arms. To the east are several Shirley family monuments from the Elizabethan period, mainly fashioned from alabaster. The rest of the church still contains fine Georgian box pews.

LEFT: *This 'Anglian Beast' is one of several examples of Anglo-Saxon sculpture from Breedon.*

BELOW LEFT: *The aisled 13th-century chancel is filled with Georgian box pews, with the Shirley aisle to the left.*

BELOW RIGHT: *The Shirley aisle has a 13th-century vault and the family pew. On the right is the extravagant tomb of Sir George Shirley (died 1598).*

ST MARY, MELTON MOWBRAY

LEICESTERSHIRE

ABOVE: *The early 14th-century west porch has ballflower details.*

BELOW: *The large crossing tower and continuous clerestory are just two of the impressive features to be found at St Mary's.*

T his fine church sits just to the south of the market-place of the important east Leicestershire town of Melton Mowbray, which in the 19th and 20th centuries was a great centre for the sport of fox hunting. Long before this, however, the town of Melton was an important medieval town, with the principal manor held by the Mowbray family, and in the later Middle Ages much wool was produced here. As a result, St Mary's was the finest parish church in the county by the early 16th century, with fourteen chantry priests as well as a vicar serving it. They lived in a communal residence to the south-east of the church, which is now called Anne of Cleves' House.

The earliest part of the church, the shell of the crossing tower, dates from the 12th century, and it was at this time that the Cluniac Priory of Lewes in East Sussex acquired a share in the manor, along with the advowson of the church. By 1285, Lewes Priory had appropriated the church and installed a vicar, and it was at this time that they rebuilt the relatively modest chancel. By contrast, the Mowbrays, assisted by other wealthy citizens of the town, started a major reconstruction of the rest of the church. The earliest visible part of this is the beautifully re-cased crossing tower and the external first stage of the tower, which displays some particularly fine late 13th-century windows.

Not long after this, a monumental rebuilding of the nave and transepts got under way. From the beginning, this was exceptionally ambitious as the transepts were given aisles on both sides, a great rarity, with three altars in each bay on the eastern side of each transept. By the early 14th century, the reconstruction was nearing completion, and a remarkable large west porch was added to the structure. This probably also contained an altar on either side, and its decoration, with elaborate niches, ballflower carving and trailing tendrils, is particularly fine.

The Black Death probably stopped any further rebuilding work, but the town was certainly flourishing again in the late 15th century, at which time the very bold decision was taken to raise the nave and transept roofs and to install a continuous clerestory all the way round. This unique feature of the church gave it 144 new upper lights, consisting of forty-eight three-light windows, which are all as distinctive on the exterior of the church as they are on the inside.

With the raising of the roofs, the tower also needed heightening, and the splendid upper stage was added at this time and given an elaborate crenellated parapet, crowned with pinnacles. On the centre of the tower is a slightly strange spirelet. The rebuilding work was completed in 1532 with the addition of a new vestry on the north side of the chancel.

ABOVE: *The clerestory windows draw the eyes upwards from the nave; the large double-aisled south transept lies in the distance.*

LEFT: *This effigy of an early 14th-century knight, probably a member of the Mowbray family, sits in a niche in the nave's south aisle.*

ST WULFRAM, GRANTHAM

LINCOLNSHIRE

ABOVE: *Henry Cheere created this monument in 1759 for Sir Dudley Ryder, the Lord Chief Justice.*

OPPOSITE: *Grantham's stunning Gothic tower and spire can be seen from far and wide.*

BELOW: *The early 14th-century crypt lies under the south aisle.*

Grantham is one of the finest parish churches in England, despite much restoration and re-furnishing in the late 19th century. The large scale rebuilding of the later 13th and the 14th centuries is one of the most magnificent at any parish church, and this culminated in the construction of one of the most beautiful towers and spires in England.

The surviving fabric still reveals evidence of the early Norman church here – for example, the herringbone work high up on the north side of the chancel and, at the very centre of the church, the beautiful late 12th-century nave piers can be seen. Then, in the 1260s, work started on a very large extension of the church to the west, which was to surround a large new tower. The sequence of building over the next century or so can be followed by looking at the window tracery.

First comes the outer wall of the north aisle, which uses the same early Gothic geometrical tracery in its windows that can be seen in Westminster Abbey and the Angel Choir at Lincoln. In the centre was a very beautiful north doorway, although this was mutilated in the early 14th century when a vaulted porch was added. By about 1300, a great gabled west front had been completed, and the magnificent, and very tall, tower was being built. This uses ballflower in its decoration, and the top stage of the tower, which runs into the spire, is particularly fine. The lowest part of the spire has tall lucarnes, and is surrounded by a series of spirelets on the corners.

This is very reminiscent of the vast tower and stone spire that were being put on Salisbury Cathedral at exactly the same time, and there is a strong connection here because Grantham Borealis (North) and Grantham Australis (South) were two of the richest prebends in Salisbury Cathedral. The church and several surrounding manors had been given to the dean and chapter of Salisbury by the king in the early Norman period.

While the spire was being completed, the south aisle was going up, and soon afterwards the south-east chapel was being built with its wonderful flowing tracery patterns. The chapel sits on a contemporary vaulted crypt, which originally had only an outside entrance. In the 15th century, a grand new staircase

ABOVE: *The late 12th-century piers are beautiful examples of Norman church architecture. Behind are George Gilbert Scott's Victorian pulpit and screen.*

was put in, leading from the chancel to the crypt.

The final stages of the enlargement of the church were not carried out until the late 15th century, when the Corpus Christi chapel was added on the north-east. Attached to its north side is the remarkable late 15th-century chantry chapel of Thomas Hall, a rich wool merchant; this is now the vestry, and sticks out at right angles to the rest of the church. The Hall family lived in the large house (now Grantham House) on the other side of the street.

The church was restored by George Gilbert Scott between 1866 and 1875. He put on the three fine new wooden roofs over the church and removed all the plaster from the walls. He also put in the rood screen, pulpit and choir stalls. The very large new reredos behind the high altar is by Sir Arthur Blomfield.

ST BOTOLPH, BOSTON

LINCOLNSHIRE

 n the late Anglo-Saxon period, Botolph, a 7th-century East Anglian monk, was a popular saint, and many new churches, including some outside several of the gates of London, for example, were dedicated to him. In Lincolnshire, at the mouth of River Witham, a whole new settlement took its name from him, as Boston is just a shortening of 'Botolph's tun'. The town was of great importance as it connected the great city of Lincoln, via the River Witham, with the Wash and the North Sea, and hence with trade to Northern Europe. The city was granted its first charter by King John in 1204, and by the late 13th century Boston was one of the most important ports in north-west Europe. This created great wealth, particularly from the wool trade, and at the beginning of the 14th century the citizens decided to celebrate this by building a vast new parish church, in the latest Decorated Gothic style.

Most of this huge new structure, with very fine curvilinear tracery in its huge windows, was completed before the Black Death. The chancel was, however, enlarged in the later 14th century, when the magnificent choir stalls were installed, and by the end of the century St Boltolph's was the largest parish church in England. It is 240 feet (73 metres) long and has an exceptionally wide aisled nave. The arcades themselves are extremely tall, and surmounted by a continuous run of fourteen large clerestory windows on each side. There was also a very fine south porch with a separate chapel to the west of it. At this time, however, the church was apparently without a tower, or perhaps retained a tower from an earlier church, as at Cley next the Sea in Norfolk (see pages 157–8).

ABOVE: *This is the effigy of Dame Margaret Tilney, who laid the first stone of Boston's steeple in 1309.*

BELOW: *The famous Boston 'stump' with the Lady chapel in the foreground.*

During the 15th century, however, the citizens of Boston surpassed themselves and put up the largest and most spectacular tower on any parish church in England. It is worth noting, however, that just up the valley at Lincoln was a cathedral with three huge towers, each capped with a spire, the central one reaching to over 450 feet (137 metres). Boston's great tower is, nevertheless, at 272 feet (83 metres) high, a truly magnificent structure, which can be seen for miles across the fenlands and out to sea. The lowest stage, which has the very large west window in it, and the re-set 14th-century west doorway beneath, are entirely covered in Perpendicular panelling. Above this is a lantern stage, with ogee tops to the windows. The vault at the top of this stage, 137 feet (42 metres) above the floor, was completed only in 1853. The third stage, for the belfry, is much plainer, with no tracery in the windows and no decoration. Finally the whole structure is topped with a wonderful openwork lantern, that is octagonal and braced with flying buttresses from the tall corner pinnacles. The lantern carries its own pinnacles and triangular filigree parapets.

The interior of the church now contains many new 19th- and 20th-century furnishings, but despite this and the many restorations, Boston's church is still as vast and fine inside as it is outside.

ABOVE: *Detail of a* c. *1390 misericord depicting a kitchen scene, found on the south side of the choir.*

LEFT: *The sanctuary at St Botolph's has a huge reredos above the high altar, which was dedicated in 1891 in memory of a seventeen-year-old who accidentally drowned.*

ST HELEN, BRANT BROUGHTON

LINCOLNSHIRE

ABOVE: *Detail of the sexpartite vault over the north porch, with animated carved bosses.*

Seven miles (11km) due east of Newark (see pages 192–3), in the flat low-lying area of south-west Lincolnshire, the superb slender spire of Brant Broughton (pronounced Bruton) can be seen. Looking carefully to the north, the dominant shape of Lincoln Minster, which once had three magnificent spires, is also visible, and to the south and west are the superb spires of Grantham (see pages 180–82) and Newark (see pages 192–3). These spires, all of which were built in the early 14th century, dominate the surrounding landscape. The spire at Brant Broughton, which is just under 200 feet (61 metres) high, is one of the finest.

There was a church on this site by the time of the Domesday Book (1086), but the earliest remaining part of the present church, the west wall, dates from the late 13th century. The two-light windows at the ends of the aisles are of this date, and the lines of the steep 13th-century pitched nave roof above the tower arch can still be seen. Of about the same date are three bays of pointed arches on either side of the nave.

By the 14th century, however, a much more splendid and elaborate rebuilding was taking place; the outer walls of the aisles were raised and crenellated, and new traceried windows were installed. Also, two very fine porches were constructed to the north and south, and all of the outside masonry was covered in exquisitely carved work, with niches, friezes, pinnacles and the like. The double sexpartite vaults within the porches are particularly fine, and it is clear that the carver-masons involved were particularly skilled. As well as this, a magnificent new west tower was built, which culminates in the tall, slender spire covered in crockets and surrounded by four crocketed spirelets. The 14th-century rebuilding work was not completed.

In the late 15th century, a fine new clerestory was installed in the nave with a shallow-pitched angel roof above it that still survives. Nothing much is known about the medieval chancel because it was

RIGHT: *The church at Brant Broughton combines a slender spire and tower, a 14th-century aisle, a 15th-century clerestory and a 19th-century chancel.*

ABOVE: *The 15th-century nave and clerestory have a stunning angel roof.*

LEFT: *The font cover dates from 1889, and opens to reveal a finely painted interior, with the figures of St Michael, St Nicholas and St Agnes.*

OPPOSITE: *Bodley's fine new chancel of 1874 has an evocative reredos at its centre, which dates from 1887.*

replaced by a new one in 1812. In 1873, however, a wealthy and artistic new rector, Canon Frederick Heathcote Sutton, came to the church. He worked with the architect G.F. Bodley to restore the church to its former glory, and for this he had a completely new chancel built between 1874 and 1876. This is a very fine Gothic Revival structure, which harmonizes well with the 14th- and 15th-century nave. Inside, it has a painted wooden lierne vault.

Much of Sutton and Bodley's re-furnishings in the church were very successful. Sutton designed much of the new stained glass himself and had it made by C.E. Kempe in a kiln at the rectory. He also designed fine new chandeliers, which were manufactured in the local forge. Other items were added after Sutton's death in 1888, including the rood screen, choir stalls and font cover in 1889–90, by Canon Arthur Sutton in memory of his uncle who was also his predecessor as rector. The chancel ceiling was restored in 1991–2.

ST JAMES, LOUTH

LINCOLNSHIRE

At just under 300 feet (91.5 metres) high, the top of the spire at St James's Church in Louth is higher than that of any other parish church in England. Because Louth is situated just north-east of the Lincolnshire Wolds, it stands out above the Wolds for the traveller approaching from the west.

The tower and spire of Louth church were added at the west end of the nave as the final stage of large-scale reconstruction work in the 14th and 15th centuries. It is clear that when the work started on the tower in the mid-15th century the tower was completely outside the church on the west, as can be seen by the massive north and south buttresses. There are, however, north and south arches into the tower, and this suggests that the intention from an early stage was to extend the nave aisles westward to flank the tower.

No early medieval masonry survives above the ground, but there must have been a big church here from at least the 12th century. Enlargement in the 13th century must also have taken place, but the earliest surviving fabric of the church, the five arches on either side of the nave, dates from the 14th century. The space between the two arcades is very wide, and it is possible they were rebuilt in the 15th century, during the main Perpendicular rebuilding.

ABOVE: *The sunburst vault is set 86 feet (26 metres) above the ground in the centre of the tower.*

ABOVE RIGHT: *Louth's wide nave dates mainly from the 15th century, but the angel roof was rebuilt in 1825.*

This rebuilding resulted in new exterior walls to the church with large windows in each of them, as well as large clerestories above the nave and chancel. The four-bay chancel must have been completely rebuilt in the 15th century, and the very large Perpendicular east window is particularly impressive. To the south of the chancel, in St Stephen's chapel, is a very fine sedilia, while the north chapel has, at its east end, some of the original choir stalls. Remarkably, the nave roof was completely rebuilt as a new angel roof in 1825, but two of the medieval angels from the earlier roof can still be observed on the east wall of the north chapel. The church was completely restored by a local architect, James Fowler, in the 1860s, and with its tiled floors, neat pews and stained glass, the interior now owes more to the 19th century than the medieval period.

Returning, finally, to the wonderful tower and spire, it has been established from churchwardens' accounts that the great three-stage structure was complete by 1499. The upper stage is a very lofty belfry above a magnificent sunburst vault. This means that the middle stage is a beautiful lantern for the western end of the church.

The spire is exceptionally tall and slender, with four 50-foot (15.25-metre) high pinnacle-spirelets round it. Between them are lace-like flying buttresses, similar to those on the Henry VII chapel at Westminster Abbey. The churchwardens' accounts tell us that the spire was started in 1501 and completed on 13 September 1515, at a total cost of £305 8s. 5d. Three separate master masons were involved, and their fees and expenses, including those for visiting the quarry, are recorded in detail. The final stage of the work was the installation of the weathercock, which was made at Lincoln from a great metal basin bought in York. It is recorded that this basin was brought to England by the 'Kyng of Scotts'.

BELOW: *This corbel supports the roof of the north nave aisle; although it dates from the 14th century it closely resembles a man using a mobile phone!*

ST MARY, STOW

LINCOLNSHIRE

ABOVE: *This 14th-century corbel showing a man playing a double wind instrument supports a stone shelf high on the east wall of the north transept.*

BELOW: *The large cruciform church at Stow has a 15th-century crossing tower.*

Some 8 miles (12.8km) north-west of Lincoln are the remains of a very important late Anglo-Saxon and Norman church. The name Stow itself signifies an important holy place, and there may have been a very early church here. However, the large central crossing and transepts at Stow date from the middle of the 11th century, and are some of the largest and best-preserved late Anglo-Saxon remains in the country. Documentary evidence suggests that Eadnoth II, who was Bishop of Dorchester-on-Thames, the vast diocese that ran from the Thames in Oxfordshire to the Humber, built the church. However, he left it unfinished at the level of the imposts on top of the crossing piers; there is evidence that a major fire occurred in the church soon after this.

In 1073, just a few years after the Norman Conquest, Remigius, the first Norman Bishop of Dorchester, moved the centre of the see to Lincoln, where he built a new cathedral. At Stow, Remigius carried on the building work, and probably completed the four large crossing arches and the nave. He may also have built a small apsidal sanctuary on the east, although only archaeological excavations below ground will answer this. Remigius was a Benedictine monk from Fécamp in Normandy, and he intended that Stow should become a monastery, introducing a few monks here in 1091. He died a year later, and his successor, Bishop Bloet, who held the see until 1123, moved the monks back to their mother house at Eynsham in Oxfordshire.

Stow was already a large estate belonging to the bishop, and it was probably Bloet and his successor, Alexander (who was bishop until 1148), who turned the church into both a parish church and a very grand bishop's chapel. They rebuilt the nave and gave it splendid south and west doorways, then followed this by putting up a magnificent three-bay vaulted chancel with splendid internal architectural decoration.

The east wall was given a new window in the 13th century, although unfortunately the vault collapsed after the Reformation. However, in 1850–52,

the Victorian architect J.L. Pearson was commissioned to rebuild the vault and to restore the east window to its original Norman form. He also put back steeply pitched roofs on the chancel, nave and transepts.

Several new windows and a fine font were added to the church in the 13th century, and a wall painting, which was rediscovered in 1865 and depicts the murder of Thomas Becket, was made in the niche above the altar in the north transept. In the 14th century, large polygonal masonry piers were installed at the four corners of the crossing, with pointed arches built above them. This was for a new crossing tower, which has a crenellated parapet and small pinnacles; inside is a ring of eight bells. No further building work was carried out on this magnificent church until the 19th-century restoration.

ABOVE: *This Anglo-Saxon doorway survives on the west side of the north transept.*

LEFT: *The east side of the crossing leads to Pearson's Victorian rib-vault and east wall in the chancel. The polygonal tower piers date from the 14th century.*

ST MARY MAGDALENE, NEWARK-ON-TRENT

NOTTINGHAMSHIRE

ABOVE: *Early 14th-century stained glass depicting Christ and Mary Magdalene.*

BELOW: *Thomas Meyring's chantry chapel sits on the north side of the sanctuary.*

ewark began its existence as a very important 12th-century castle belonging to the Bishop of Lincoln and situated on the south-east side of the River Trent, where the Fosse Way met the Great North Road (now the A1). South-east of the castle a triangular market-place was created, and beside this a large new parish church was built in the late 12th century. All that remains of this first church are parts of the crossing piers and a small two-bay rib-vaulted crypt under the sanctuary.

By the early 13th century, a long nave had been built and a large new west tower was going up, which superseded the crossing tower. This tower still contains a fine west doorway, and at the top of its third stage is a trellis-pattern decoration that is identical to that used at Lincoln Minster. Above this was added a fine new belfry in the elaborate style of the early 14th century and, to cap the whole lot, a magnificent stone spire that rises to 252 feet (77 metres) above the ground, which can be seen for many miles. It was clearly competing with the even taller stone spire at Grantham (see pages 180–82), 14 miles (22.5km) down the Great North Road from Newark.

While the spire was going up, we know that by 1312 work was in progress on a magnificent new south aisle to the nave. This has large windows with fine flowing tracery patterns in them.

In the late Middle Ages, Newark was a relatively small but very wealthy town, thanks to sheep and the wool trade. This is now best shown by the vast monumental brass in the church that is dedicated to Alan Fleming, a Newark merchant of foreign origin who died in 1363. Fleming founded the Corpus Christi Chantry Chapel in the church in 1349, the year the Black Death struck this region.

The rest of the rebuilding of this huge parish church took place in the second half of the 15th century, and is in the mature Perpendicular style. The nave itself and the north aisle were rebuilt with a large clerestory, and a new south porch was squashed in to fit within the market boundary. The eastern arm, however, had more room, and this was rebuilt on a very large scale with tall, light-filled transepts and extremely wide aisles. Beyond the high altar was an ambulatory with an eastern Lady chapel and two very large chapels on either side, each having huge east windows, a reflection of the colossal east end of York Minster. The building work was complete by 1498, and the interior was then sumptuously furnished. The choir still contains its screens and twenty-six stalls with carved misericords dating from about 1500. On either side of the sanctuary are two small chantry chapels within stone screens for the wealthy Meyring and Markham families. In his will of 1500, Thomas Meyring directed that 'all [his] clipped wool and all [his] floke of sheep' be sold to pay for his chantry.

ABOVE: *Early 16th-century figures, which include the 'dance of death', decorate the openings to the Markham chantry on the south side of the sanctuary.*

RIGHT: *The church's ornate tower and spire date from the early 14th century, and appear to have been built in competition with the taller spire at Grantham.*

193

THE NORTHERN COUNTIES

This area has the most diverse group of churches in all of England. There are some exceptionally early survivals and even a church that was almost certainly built for a king. Patrington and Nantwich are two of the most beautiful 14th-century churches in England, while Berwick is a very rare mid-17th century church. Finally there are oddities, such as Tamworth's double spiral staircase and Chesterfield's crooked spire.

RIGHT: *The crowded churchyard at Bewcastle, with its exceptional Anglo-Saxon cross-shaft.*

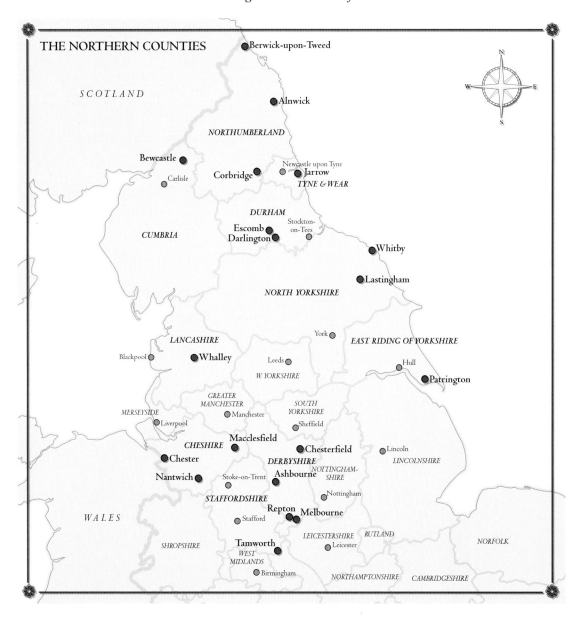

THE NORTHERN COUNTIES

- Berwick-upon-Tweed
- SCOTLAND
- Alnwick
- NORTHUMBERLAND
- Bewcastle
- Carlisle
- Corbridge
- Newcastle upon Tyne
- Jarrow
- TYNE & WEAR
- DURHAM
- Escomb
- Stockton-on-Tees
- CUMBRIA
- Darlington
- Whitby
- Lastingham
- NORTH YORKSHIRE
- LANCASHIRE
- York
- EAST RIDING OF YORKSHIRE
- Blackpool
- Whalley
- Leeds
- Hull
- W. YORKSHIRE
- Patrington
- GREATER MANCHESTER
- SOUTH YORKSHIRE
- MERSEYSIDE
- Manchester
- Liverpool
- Sheffield
- CHESHIRE
- Macclesfield
- Chesterfield
- Lincoln
- Chester
- DERBYSHIRE
- LINCOLNSHIRE
- Nantwich
- Stoke-on-Trent
- Ashbourne
- NOTTINGHAM-SHIRE
- Nottingham
- STAFFORDSHIRE
- Repton
- Melbourne
- WALES
- Stafford
- LEICESTERSHIRE
- RUTLAND
- NORFOLK
- SHROPSHIRE
- Tamworth
- Leicester
- WEST MIDLANDS
- Birmingham
- NORTHAMPTONSHIRE
- CAMBRIDGESHIRE

ST EDITHA, TAMWORTH

STAFFORDSHIRE

ABOVE: *Glass designed by Edward Burne-Jones sits in the east window of St George's chapel.*

BELOW: *Early 14th-century tomb recesses on the north side of the aisle have Freville and Ferrers tombs within them.*

I n the 8th century Tamworth was a residence for the Mercian royal family, and in AD 913 a burh – a Saxon fortified town – was created here to repel the Vikings. At the centre of this town, which sits on the border between Warwickshire and Staffordshire, is the church of St Editha, which was probably first built in the 10th century. St Editha, who was the sister of King Athelstan, was given in marriage in AD 926 to the pagan Scandinavian king, Sihtric, at Tamworth. The earliest church here was destroyed later in the 10th century and rebuilt by King Edgar, who reigned between 959 and 975, but whether any of the surviving masonry at the core of the church dates from this time is unknown.

RIGHT: *The great west tower must once have been capped by a central spire.*

OPPOSITE RIGHT: *The fine late 17th-century monument to Sir John Ferrers (died 1680) can be found on the north side of the porch, below the tower.*

After the Norman Conquest, a castle and a new market-place were built to the south-west of the church, above the meeting point of the River Tame and River Anker, and the church itself was rebuilt as a large cruciform structure. At its centre was a large tower, and the early 12th-century round arches on either side of this still survive. They are decorated with chevron ornaments and billet-moulded hoods. The south wall of the chancel is also still in part 12th-century.

The nave was given wide aisles in the 13th century, at a time when the town was growing rapidly, and beneath the south aisle is a fine vaulted crypt. A major fire gutted the church on 23 May 1345, which led to the complete rebuilding of the nave, aisles and transepts.

At the end of the 14th century the chapel of St George was added on the north-east, and between it and the chancel are three fine tombs belonging to the Frevilles and Ferrers, who held Tamworth Castle at this time. The chancel was also rebuilt in the late 14th century with clerestory windows at its east end. In the 15th century the clerestory was extended for the full length of the chancel and nave, and a magnificent tower was added at the west end. This was probably meant to have a large central spire, as well as its four spirelets. Uniquely the tower has a double spiral staircase in its south-west corner, with separate entrances outside and inside the church.

Throughout the later Middle Ages the church was collegiate, with a dean and five canons. Their stalls and those of the vicars would have sat beneath the Norman arches in the crossing. The college was abolished in 1547, and the present furnishings of the church date mainly from the restorations of 1869–71, although the iron screen at the entrance to the chancel was installed in the 18th century. St Editha's contains much fine Victorian stained glass, by such luminaries as the pre-Raphaelite artist Edward Burne-Jones and the famed designer William Morris (1834–96).

ST MICHAEL AND ST MARY, MELBOURNE

DERBYSHIRE

ABOVE: *The hatchment of Lord Melbourne, Queen Victoria's first prime minister, hangs on the south wall of the chancel.*

BELOW: *The 15th-century chancel, with the arched west wall of the otherwise demolished upper chapel of St Nicholas above it.*

elbourne lies in a prominent position just to the south of the River Trent. In the 12th century this river formed a strategic frontier between northern and southern England. Melbourne's magnificent unfinished church was built on a very grand scale for Henry I in the 1120s, probably by his chaplain and confessor Athelwold (or Adelulf), who was an Augustinian canon and Prior of both Nostell in Yorkshire and Carlisle. In 1133, Athelwold was also consecrated as the first bishop of Carlisle, and the king gave him the church at Melbourne as part of the endowment of the new see. Melbourne was always a royal manor, but the Bishop of Carlisle also retained an important residence here in the late Middle Ages, which was used on the long journey between London and Carlisle.

The magnificent church at Melbourne was built with a five-bay, aisled nave and large transepts. To the east were three apsidal chapels, the central one, most unusually, was constructed with two storeys, which accounts for the church's double dedication – the altar of St Michael was in the upper chapel. Sadly, the upper chapel was demolished in the late Middle Ages, and the chancel was then made square ended and given a new roof and east window. The apsidal chapels on either side were demolished even earlier, probably in the 14th century.

As originally planned, the church was intended to have three large towers, none of which was completed above roof level; the west front is particularly diminished by this on the exterior. The upper part of the central crossing tower dates only from the 17th century. Within the church, however, the grandiose architecture, with its great chevron Norman arches, is still very apparent. A very rare feature is the large west gallery on a groined vault, which was almost certainly constructed for the king. From here, Henry and his retainers could walk along the clerestory passages to more passages within the walls of the crossing tower, which connected to the private upper chapel of St Michael. This type of Romanesque magnificence was more likely to be found in Imperial Germany than England at this time, and it is perhaps no coincidence that Henry I planned to make his daughter Matilda (1102–67), and her husband, Henry V of Germany, the Holy Roman Emperor, his heirs. Henry died in 1135

RIGHT: *The great aisled nave looking east, with the bell-ropes hanging down into the crossing.*

BELOW: *In the remains of a wall painting, a devil hovers over two women who are arguing over a cup. The painting can be seen in the distance on the west face of the north-west crossing pier in the picture to the right.*

and the 12th-century elements of the church at Melbourne were left unfinished. Even the south clerestory of the nave was left incomplete, and, as can be seen from the architecture, it was not completed until the early 1200s.

In the 13th century, the church became an ordinary parish church, and by the late Middle Ages the aisles were heightened and given new windows. The chancel was rebuilt, as we have seen, and a new roof was put on the nave. The church's great imperial days were long gone. However, in the 1840s, Lord Melbourne, Queen Victoria's first prime minister, inhabited the large house near the church and it was he who gave his name to the great city in Australia.

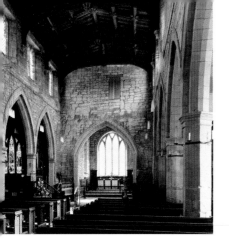

ST WYSTAN, REPTON

DERBYSHIRE

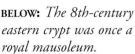

ABOVE: *The nave looking east to the Anglo-Saxon chancel.*

BELOW: *The 8th-century eastern crypt was once a royal mausoleum.*

S ituated on the south bank of the River Trent, next to a famous school, the parish church at Repton appears, at first sight, to be just another fine late medieval church with a slender spire. The cruciform eastern end of the church, however, incorporates some fascinating Anglo-Saxon remains, and below the chancel is one of the most important early crypts in England, which on closer examination reveals itself as a royal mausoleum.

A monastery was first founded at Repton before the end of the 7th century; headed by an abbess, this institution became an early 'mission station' in pagan Mercia. The Anglo-Saxon Chronicle records that when King Ethelbald of Mercia was killed in AD 757, he was buried 'at Repton', as was King Wiglaf in AD 839. Wiglaf's grandson, Wystan, who was later made a saint, was murdered in AD 849, and it is recorded that he 'was buried in the mausoleum of his grandfather Wiglaf in the famous monastery at Repton'. Modern scholarship has indicated that the mausoleum must be the eastern crypt, which can be entered by two long, narrow, stepped passageways on the eastern side of the church. The crypt itself still contains four free-standing columns in the centre, with recesses round the edges. The royal burials have long gone, but the shrine of St Wystan was probably placed either in the centre or on the western side of the crypt.

The Anglo-Saxon Chronicle also tells us that the great Viking army spent the winter of AD 873–4 at Repton. Amazingly, recent archaeological excavations have found clear evidence of their winter camp within a great bank and ditch, which incorporated the church on the south.

After the Norman Conquest, the church was rebuilt. In the 1150s, a new Augustinian priory was constructed immediately to the east of the church, which now houses Repton School. In the 13th century, the nave was given aisles, and in the early 14th century, the nave and aisles were rebuilt in their present form with fine arcades and new windows in the outer walls. The eastern pointed arches were constructed only in the 19th century, replacing the Anglo-Saxon round-headed arches. A new south porch and south-east chapel were also created in the 14th century, followed in the next century by a new west tower and tall thin spire that rose to 212 feet (64.6 metres) above the ground. The final major work was the construction of the castellated clerestory, with a new timber roof, above the nave and choir. Luckily, the small, square Anglo-Saxon sanctuary at the eastern end of the church, which was reopened only in the 1940s, was left intact, although some new windows were inserted here, including a lancet on the south. Since the archaeological excavations of the 1970s and 1980s, the ground level around the eastern crypt has once again been lowered, and the remarkable 8th-century stone plinth of the crypt can be clearly seen.

OPPOSITE: *Repton's 15th-century spire is impressively slender, as seen here from the south side of the church.*

ST OSWALD, ASHBOURNE

DERBYSHIRE

ABOVE: *This white marble monument to five-year-old Penelope Boothby (died 1791) was made in 1793 by Thomas Banks; Penelope was the sitter for Sir Joshua Reynolds's famous portrait* The Little Girl in the Mob Cap.

BELOW: *The great, 212-foot (64.6-metre) spire, as seen from the south, with a glimpse of the south transept through the trees.*

ituated at the southern end of the Derbyshire Dales, Ashbourne has the finest parish church in the county. Despite possessing a magnificent spire, which is 212 feet (64.6 metres) high, St Oswald's is not particularly prominent from a distance, because it is sited low down on the western side of the town. Ashbourne was given its market charter in 1257, and at the same time the town's parish church was rebuilt on a grand scale. A very rare survival is the church's original brass dedicatory inscription, now displayed in the south transept, which tells us that Hugh de Patishul, Bishop of Coventry, dedicated the church in 1241. This was probably the date that the eastern arm of the church, with its very long chancel, transepts and large eastern chapels, was completed. The chancel not only contained a fine eastern sanctuary, but also grand stalls for priests at its western end. The priests were able to enter the chancel directly via a magnificent doorway on the south, which is still flanked by early 13th-century lancet windows.

The people's part of the church – the nave – was always modest by contrast. Although it did receive a large south aisle in the early 14th century, a north aisle was never built. There is fine Decorated window tracery in the south aisle, and in the late Middle Ages a clerestory was added,

filling the space with more light. Remarkably, there is also a clerestory on the eastern side of the north transept. Other, larger, windows were also put into the church in the late medieval period, and these now contain much fine Victorian glass.

The church belonged to the dean and chapter of Lincoln for most of the Middle Ages. It may have been this body that encouraged the building of a fine new crossing tower and spire in the early 14th century, when they were also completing the tallest crossing tower and spire in the world at Lincoln Minster.

The large transept chapels at St Oswald's, which functioned as family chantries in the later medieval period, are exceptional. To the north was the Lady chapel, founded as a new chantry in 1391. By the 15th century, a prominent local family, the Cockaynes, were installing fine monuments in the chapel – it is likely that they built the clerestory and new roof above. From the late 17th century, the Boothbys of Ashbourne Hall took over the north transept as 'their' chapel, adding more grand monuments.

The church was restored by George Gilbert Scott between 1876 and 1878, at which time it was given many new furnishings.

LEFT: *A large Perpendicular east window of the 1390s floods the 13th-century chancel with light. The chancel was redecorated in 1963 by Stephen Dykes Bower.*

BELOW: *The Boothby chapel is filled with monuments to the Cockayne family; this is a detail from the tomb of Sir John Cockayne (died 1447) and his wife, Margaret. Both the Boothbys and the Cockaynes were powerful local families.*

ST MARY AND ALL SAINTS, CHESTERFIELD

DERBYSHIRE

ABOVE: *Detail from the high altar reredos of 1898 by Temple Moore, which was coloured in 1936.*

BELOW: *The large aisled nave has slender early 14th-century arcades.*

T he large parish church of St Mary and All Saints in the centre of Chesterfield is most famous for its crooked spire. The site of the town is ancient – on the top of the hill, above the River Rother where the church stands, a Roman fort was built in the 1st century AD. An Anglo-Saxon town later occupied the site and the settlement expanded greatly in the early 13th century when a large new market-place was created. There must have been an Anglo-Saxon church here, but it was completely replaced in the later Middle Ages. The worn tub-font in the south transept is probably Norman.

RIGHT: *The famous twisted, leaning wood and lead spire of St Mary and All Saints is now considered to be relatively stable.*

BELOW: *This shows the effigy of Thomas Foljambe (died 1604), the 13-year-old great-grandson of Sir Henry Foljambe, on whose tomb he kneels. The helm is a diminutive replacement of the original, which was struck off during the Commonwealth.*

The rebuilding of the church on its present scale started in the 13th century, and some fragments dating back to this period still survive, for example the trefoil-headed piscina in the Holy Cross chapel. The first of the town's guilds, the Holy Cross Guild, was founded in 1218 and it was this and other similar organizations that raised much additional money for the fine

rebuilding of the church in the first half of the 14th century. A beautiful new aisled nave was built, with an exceptional great west window and a porch on the south-west. The eastern arm beyond the transepts was also rebuilt, with the chancel flanked by large new chapels of St Katherine to the north and St Mary to the south. Outer chapels entered from the transepts were also built, and the so-called Lesser Lady chapel to the south is very unusual in England as it has a polygonal east end.

Central to all this reconstruction work was the substantial crossing tower, with a large belfry in its upper stage. On top of this sits the so-called 'crooked spire'. This structure, which is made from timber and covered in lead, was built in the 1360s. It was made in twelve separate stages, each of which was slightly rotated to give a spiral effect. Unfortunately, some of the timbers in the frames have distorted over time, giving a distinct lean to the south-west. Many later timbers were installed and the top 25 feet (7.6 metres) of the spire were completely rebuilt in 1951 – it is now relatively stable.

At the eastern end of the Lady chapel, to the south of the high altar, is a magnificent collection of 16th-century tombs relating to the Foljambe family. Particularly fine is the monument to Henry Foljambe, who died in 1510, and his wife. It has an alabaster tomb-chest, which was made at Burton-on-Trent and cost £10. Nearby are several late 16th-century monuments to other members of the family, which were made by Dutch artists. To the west of the chapel is a beautiful screen, which dates from about 1500, and retains its coved-out top for a rood loft.

ABOVE: *The timbers in the spire were set in a spiral in the 14th century.*

LEFT: *The Reynolds window in the north wall of St Katherine's chapel was made in 1957 by Christopher Webb.*

ST MICHAEL, MACCLESFIELD

CHESHIRE

O n the western side of the Peak District lies the attractive east Cheshire town of Macclesfield. As a medieval town it received its first charter in 1261, but from the mid-18th century it was most famous for its silk mills. The centre of the town is on a ridge with a high street running south–north and a market-place in the middle. The church is to the east, with a very steep drop beyond its east end.

Documentary evidence tells us that a new church was consecrated in 1278, but very little of this building now survives. There is enough, however, to tell us that the present south aisle was originally the nave, and the deeply moulded 13th-century capitals for the nave arcade still exist. To this nave was added a Perpendicular west tower – now the south-west tower – and some of its external masonry survives. Inside, its original tower arch can be seen, along with the tierceron vault and central bell-hole below the ringing chamber. The one other area of the pre-Reformation church to survive is the Savage chapel on the south side. This is a two-bay structure with a remarkable three-storey porch on the west. To the west of it was the early 15th-century Legh chapel, which was rebuilt in 1620. The rest of the church was apparently rebuilt between 1739 and 1740, although this church was also demolished and completely rebuilt between 1898 and 1901 to the Victorian Gothic designs of Sir Arthur Blomfield. It is this church that now occupies most of the northern part of the space. It was filled with stained glass by Kempe and Powell, which even now is barely a century old. There is also much glass by William Morris, and the east window, which was designed by Edward Burne-Jones, was made in 1905.

Macclesfield's church is now most famous for its monuments, and has the best collection in Cheshire. Many of these are for members of the Savage family, and they can be found in the chancel and the Savage chapel. Most are made of alabaster, and one can follow the evolution of the monuments from about 1475 to the early 17th century. Confusingly, many of the male members of the family are called John Savage. The most famous member of the family was Thomas Savage, Archbishop of York from 1501 to 1507,

ABOVE: *A detail of an angel between two wide tomb-niches.*

BELOW: *The blackened sandstone, late medieval, Perpendicular west tower, as seen from the south-west.*

RIGHT: *The fine east window contains glass designed by Edward Burne-Jones.*

who built the chapel. His fine monument is, however, in the north choir aisle at York Minster. Against the west wall of the chapel is the famous 'Pardon' brass for Roger Legh, who died in 1506. Part of the brass is missing, but on the left is Legh with six sons behind him. In the centre the inscription says that 'the pardon for the saying of five Paternosters, five Aves and a creed is 26 thousand years and 26 days of pardon'.

RIGHT: *The excellent effigy of Thomas, Earl Rivers (died 1694), who was also known as Viscount Colchester and Savage of Rocksavage, was made in 1696 by William Staunton; it can be found in the south aisle.*

ST MARY, NANTWICH

CHESHIRE

antwich, in southern Cheshire, was once a major centre for the salt industry. The town first flourished in the Roman period and then from Anglo-Saxon times until the late 16th century. The church of St Mary, which is the finest in Cheshire, is in the middle of the town and did not legally become the parish church until the 17th century. Before this it was merely a 'chapel of ease' for Acton parish church, which is just outside Nantwich to the north-west.

The magnificent church is a large cruciform building with an aisle-less chancel and transepts, a four-bay aisled nave and vaulted south porch. Crowning the whole building is a splendid octagonal bell-tower above the crossing. The chancel was rebuilt in a most impressive way in the mid-14th century, with large traceried windows and a superb lierne-vault covered in bosses. This is very unusual in a mere parish church, let alone a chapel of ease. Almost all the decorative details, including the vestry on the north, suggest a date before the mid-14th century. The east window, which has a wonderful open-work ogee arch above it on the exterior, is filled with pure Perpendicular tracery, suggesting a late 14th-century date. Presumably, this replaced the original tracery, but why this was done is unknown.

Also dating from the late 14th century are the impressive canopied choir stalls. Twenty of them contain seats with splendidly carved misericords, and all depict non-Christian scenes, such as dragons, a mermaid, wrestlers, a pelican, and a wife beating her husband with a ladle. In the crossing outside the chancel is a magnificent stone pulpit covered in panelling. The church also has a wooden pulpit dating from 1601 in the nave.

The church was restored by

ABOVE: *Tomb of Sir Thomas Smith of Hough (died 1614) and his wife, Anne.*

BELOW: *The vaulted chancel and its Perpendicular east window can be seen from the lofty nave.*

George Gilbert Scott between 1854 and 1861, and, most unfortunately, he mutilated the west front by replacing the Perpendicular and Decorated doorway with work in a late 13th-century style – a phase the Victorians called 'second pointed'. Scott also put in a black-and-red lierne vault above the crossing. Despite this, Nantwich is one of the most splendid 14th-century buildings in the whole of north-west England.

BELOW LEFT: *The magnificent 14th-century octagonal tower over the crossing, with the 15th-century clerestory beneath.*

BELOW: *The amusing carvings on the misericords at St Mary's include details of a hunting fox and wrestlers.*

ST JOHN THE BAPTIST, CHESTER

CHESHIRE

his now slightly sad church was once of very great importance, and for a time was the cathedral for Chester – the present cathedral has only been such since 1541. The large building that survives has lost both its east and west ends, although parts of the ruins of the former can still be seen outside the Victorian east wall of the church. On the north-west was a massive late-medieval bell-tower, but this crashed down in 1881 and destroyed the very fine 13th-century porch. The porch was rebuilt in 1882, and a new north-east bell-tower was put up between 1886 and 1887, beside the crossing.

The earliest church on this site was built on the eastern side of the large Roman amphitheatre,

ABOVE: *A detail from the 1889 west window shows King Edgar being rowed on the River Dee by eight 'kings' in* AD *973.*

BELOW: *The late Victorian north side of the church with the early Gothic clerestory above.*

possibly in the 7th century. By the late Anglo-Saxon period, it was an important church in a separate quarter outside the city walls, known as the Bishop's Borough. The owner was the Bishop of Lichfield, and in 1075 a Norman bishop named Peter moved his cathedral to St John's. The cathedral only remained here for about twenty years, and the Norman core of the present building was not put up until the years after 1100, by which time the cathedral had moved to a rich monastery at Coventry.

The eastern end of the present church still retains the fine large crossing piers of the early Norman church and fragments of the contemporary architecture around it. One can also see the eastern part of the large aisled nave with circular pillars and round-headed arches. At the eastern end of the church were three apsidal chapels, but the ruins of the west wall of this part are all that survive, with fragments of rebuilt 14th-century chapels beyond. Work on building the upper part of the nave ceased quite early on, presumably because the money was being used for the two other new Romanesque cathedrals in the diocese, Coventry and Lichfield. At the end of the 12th century, however, work continued and beautiful triforium arcades were built in the nave. After another pause, no doubt during King John's chaotic reign, the clerestories were built in the full early Gothic style with stiff-leaf capitals.

Not much else of the medieval church survives, although the stump of the massive north-west bell-tower indicates that it was still an important church in the late Middle Ages.

With the making of the new cathedral at the old Benedictine monastery of St Werburgh, within the city walls, St John's was allowed to decline and fall into a ruined state. It was only in the late 19th century that major restoration work was carried out, although it is sad that the north-west tower could not have been saved from collapsing in 1881.

Here is a rare example of a church that could perhaps be enlarged again in the 21st century by rebuilding its eastern arm and reincorporating it into the church.

ABOVE LEFT: *Ruins of the original east end of the church can still be seen.*

LEFT: *The Norman nave arcade has a fine late 12th-century triforium arcade above.*

ST MARY, WHALLEY

LANCASHIRE

Whalley is still centred round its parish church and the remains of a large Cistercian abbey. The first stone for a new abbey church was not laid until 1330, because the earlier abbey had been situated in the Wirral peninsula at Stanlow. It was constantly being flooded, so, once they had acquired the surrounding land in 1296, about twenty monks moved to the rectory house beside Whalley parish church. In the 14th and 15th centuries, the monks built a large new complex of buildings near the church.

After his involvement in the Pilgrimage of Grace, the abbot was executed in 1537 and the abbey was forfeited to Henry VIII as part of the Dissolution of the Monasteries. The abbot had just built a fine house for himself, which still survives in part. The abbey church was demolished, and the monks' stalls were removed to the parish church, and, along with their splendid canopies, they are now one of the glories of the building and can be seen in the chancel. The

chancel itself dates from the 13th century, as can be seen by the lancet windows between large external buttresses.

To the west are the aisled nave and an oblong tower. The nave contains much fine woodwork, including a panelled west gallery with the organ and the churchwardens' and constable's pews, which date to 1638. There is also the rectory pew, which dates from 1702, and an amazing confection called 'The Cage', which was built in 1697 from various earlier bits of woodwork. The Cage was fought over for years by the Fort and Taylor families – their initials are over the two doors – and eventually a consistory (ecclesiastical) court ruled that they should both occupy it. This squabble highlights the great importance of private family pews in the period between the 17th and mid-19th centuries. It was a time when a family and its servants spent much time in church, and their pews (which, at their grandest, often formed an enclosed and very private space with a fireplace), were an extension of their nearby houses.

A worthy recent addition to the church is the reredos, carved by George Jack in 1928.

In the churchyard, to the south of the church, are the remains of three important Anglo-Saxon crosses that must be over 1,000 years old. They indicate that Whalley was an important Christian centre in Lancashire well before the Norman Conquest, and there is likely to have been a church here from at least the 10th century.

BELOW: *The nave has a fine timber roof and rectory pew.*

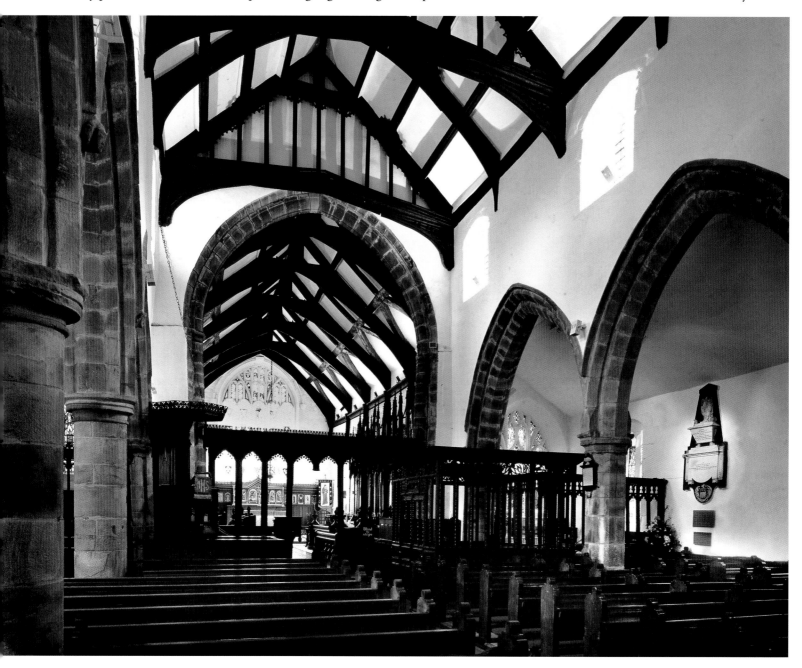

ST PATRICK, PATRINGTON
YORKSHIRE (EAST RIDING)

T his building is surely the most beautiful early 14th-century Decorated parish church in England, but sadly we know very little about its constructional history. The manor belonged to the archbishops of York, who assigned the church to the canons of the Minster of St John in Beverley with their provost holding the advowson. A will made by Robert de Patrington in 1349, while he was the Precentor of York Minster, requested that his body be buried in Patrington church. He later became Treasurer of York Minster and lived until 1371. It is possible that he was also the principal investor in this marvellous church. It is also worth noting that another Robert de Patrington became master mason at York Minster in 1368.

Patrington is situated in Holderness, in the south-east corner of the East Riding. The area to the north of the Humber estuary was a rich agricultural area when the church was built, and there are several other fine churches in the area, for example at Hedon and Howden. The greatest of all, though, is Beverley Minster.

At first glance, Patrington's church appears to be entirely of one period – the early 14th century. However, it is clear that the beautiful 180-foot (60-metre) spire was completed in the later 14th century, as was the Perpendicular east window. The form of the building and some of its detailing suggest that the nave's ground plan harks back to the 13th century, with the old foundations being reused. The extreme north-west pier in the nave also contains reused 13th-century moulded stones in its foundation. The basic form of the building follows that of

ABOVE: *Grotesque heads leer down from the north-east corner of the south transept.*

BELOW: *St Patrick's spacious crossing and the late 14th-century east window in the distance.*

ABOVE LEFT: *Intricately carved foliage on a capital.*

ABOVE RIGHT: *Carved sheep, such as in this corbel beside the door to the north transept, appear all over the church.*

ABOVE: *A detail of the Easter sculpture, with Jesus rising out of his tomb and being censed by an angel.*

OPPOSITE: *Patrington's wonderful architecture is best seen from the south-east side of the churchyard.*

such great buildings as York and Beverley Minsters, but on a smaller scale. The use of the aisles on both sides of the transepts as well as for the nave is, however, exceptional for a parish church. Only the chancel is not aisled, but this was built wider than its predecessor, as can be seen by the curved walls at its western end.

Also quite exceptional is the stone vaulting of the aisles, although this was not completed in the north transept. Highly unusual, too, is the polygonal shape of the centre chapel on the east side of the south transept. There are many fine decorative details in the church, but most interesting are the superb Easter sepulchre and sedilia on the north and south sides of the chancel. In the Easter sepulchre Jesus can be seen climbing out of a tomb, while being censed by angels. Below are three sleeping soldiers.

One slight oddity in the construction of the church is its exceptionally plain tower, which has no decorative work. Perhaps this was built in the period after the Black Death of 1348–9, during which many of the masons may have died.

The church was restored between 1885 and 1886 and given a new roof by the Reverend Henry Maddock, a canon of York Minster, but it was not until 1936 that a new gilded Gothic reredos, fashioned by J. Harold Gibbons, was put in.

Despite all its wonderful detail, it is the overall form of the building that makes this the finest Decorated church in England.

ST MARY, LASTINGHAM

NORTH YORKSHIRE

ABOVE: *Detail of St Chad in the Victorian glass of the north aisle, dedicated to the mother of Ann Ringer, a little girl from London who died during her birthday party while staying at Lastingham and to whose memory almost all the glass in St Mary's is dedicated.*

BELOW: *The church as seen from the south, with the North Yorkshire moors beyond.*

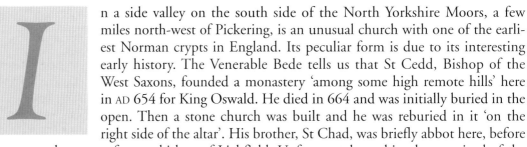

I n a side valley on the south side of the North Yorkshire Moors, a few miles north-west of Pickering, is an unusual church with one of the earliest Norman crypts in England. Its peculiar form is due to its interesting early history. The Venerable Bede tells us that St Cedd, Bishop of the West Saxons, founded a monastery 'among some high remote hills' here in AD 654 for King Oswald. He died in 664 and was initially buried in the open. Then a stone church was built and he was reburied in it 'on the right side of the altar'. His brother, St Chad, was briefly abbot here, before moving on to become a famous bishop of Lichfield. Unfortunately nothing has survived of the Anglo-Saxon church, as it was probably destroyed by the Vikings in the 9th century. There are, however, some fine fragments of Anglo-Saxon sculpture in the crypt, including part of a very large crosshead. There is also a Danish 'hogback' tombstone dating from the 10th century, which suggests that Christianity was re-established here well before the Norman conquest.

In 1078, William I permitted Stephen, the abbot of the recently re-founded monastery at Whitby, to take a group of Benedictine monks and re-establish the monastery at Lastingham. What they built over the next ten years forms the shell of the present church. With a downhill

slope from west to east, they started with a square groin-vaulted crypt with four large piers in it. To the east was a small apsidal sanctuary, which still has its original barrel vaults. This crypt, which was originally entered from a vaulted passage to the north, is still completely intact, forming a remarkable example of 11th-century architecture. Above the crypt the eastern end of a new monastic church was also built with an apsidal sanctuary and the space to the west for the monks' choir. Above this a crossing tower was planned, as can be seen from the surviving shell. Nothing further was done, as the monks moved to York in 1088. The church remained the property of St Mary's Abbey in York, and it was formally made a parish church in 1228. Simple aisles were then made on either side – the inserted 13th-century arcades can still be seen – and a new west wall was constructed. The south aisle was enlarged in the early 14th century, and a small west tower was added in the 15th century.

In 1879 the church was thoroughly restored by the well-known Victorian architect, J.L. Pearson. Unfortunately, as was his wont, he over-restored the building and put in new groin-vaults and clerestory windows. The building now contains much late 19th-century masonry, as well as its cruder, but very impressive 11th-century work.

ABOVE: *The apsidal end of the crypt, with a late 11th-century capital in the foreground.*

BELOW: *Thirteenth-century arcades line the length of the nave.*

ST MARY, WHITBY

NORTH YORKSHIRE

Whitby's parish church is now one of the most famous churches in England, largely because it escaped restoration in the Victorian period. In the early 19th century, many churches in England would have been filled with galleries, box pews and a triple-decker pulpit, as at Whitby, but virtually all of them were gutted as part of the great Christian revival of the late 19th century.

On the clifftops of Whitby, high above the mouth of the River Esk on the North Yorkshire coast, St Hilda (AD 614–80), the Abbess of Hartlepool, founded a major new abbey in AD 657. In AD 664, the abbey was the scene of the famous church Synod that discussed the calculation of the date of Easter. The Roman method, as opposed to that used by the Celts, was decided upon, and from that point until the 16th-century Dissolution of the Monasteries the Church of Rome dominated English Christianity. Whitby Abbey, which became an important centre of learning and a royal burial place, was destroyed by the Vikings in AD 867. By the late 11th century it flourished again, and the dramatic 13th- and

early 14th-century ruins of the abbey's church, which tower over the parish church, show what a powerful institution it was in the Middle Ages. Sadly the great abbey collapsed in stages during the later heyday of the parish church, with the nave falling in 1762, followed the next year by the south transept. Most of the west front fell in 1794, followed by the crossing tower in 1830.

The parish church was probably first erected in the mid-12th century and, despite all the later interventions, much survives of the shell of its original nave and chancel, including the large, moulded chancel arch. Externally, the south door-way and traces of its porch's roofline also survive. The large squat tower on the western side was added in the late 12th century, and traces of 13th-century modifications can be seen in the eastern end of the church and the transepts. The church's exterior is dominated by a whole series of domestic windows and external staircases to the galleries, which were put in during the 18th century. The two very shallow pitched gables and the row of eight lancet windows on the north side even suggest the façade of a non-conformist chapel.

The interior of the church is a magnificent example of a post-Reformation auditory church – a church focused on the pulpit and arranged so that as many people as possible can hear and see the preacher. At Whitby the centre of the church is still the fine triple-decker pulpit, which was built in 1778, although it was moved to its present position in 1847. Beneath this are the vicarage pew and a stove, and all around are box pews for the ordinary parishioners. Looking down over these are the galleries, where the community's most important members once sat. Whitby's galleries are a delightful remnant from the Age of Reason. Most of them are well-lit by back lights, top lights and even dormer windows in the roof. The most important gallery is the Cholmley Pew, which runs across the chancel arch, behind the pulpit. Richard Cholmley acquired the site in 1540, and in the 17th century the Cholmleys built the very grand Abbey House to the south-east of the church. The ruined shell of the banqueting house has just been turned into a new visitor centre by English Heritage.

BELOW: *The large graveyard spreads out far and wide from the church, which stands majestically above the town of Whitby.*

ST CUTHBERT, DARLINGTON

COUNTY DURHAM

Until the 19th century, the market town of Darlington was owned and controlled by the bishops of Durham. Then, in 1825, the famous Stockton and Darlington railway was built and the town expanded rapidly. Before this, the town was just based around a large market square, with the parish church to the east of it. Beyond this is the River Skerne, while to the south, where the ugly 1970s town hall and car park are situated, was the bishop's manor house.

Some fragments of sculpture and the survival of a Viking hogback tombstone suggest that there was an earlier, late Anglo-Saxon church on this site. However, it was Bishop Hugh le Puiset (1125–95), or Pudsey as he was later called, who began work on the present building in 1192. From the beginning, it was created as a large collegiate church with transepts and an aisled nave, and it remains one of the most important Early English churches in the north of the country. The first elements to be built were the chancel and lower part of the south transept, where the elaborate Transitional architecture can be seen, with much fine carved stiff-leaf decoration on the capitals and nailhead in the arches. It was perhaps the intention to include vaults, but this never happened.

After the chaos of King John's reign, the rest of the church was finished in the early 13th century with plainer architectural decoration. However, the aisled nave was cleverly built with more

elaborate piers at the east end, followed by alternating round and octagonal pillars to the west. In the early 14th century, the tower and the spire were built, but settlement problems meant that a large pulpitum (screen) arch had to be built and strengthening work had to take place below the east side of the tower in the 15th century. The spire was rebuilt in 1752, and a large organ was put on top of the pulpitum later.

The church was not enlarged in the later Middle Ages, but the nave aisles were heightened in the 14th century and large, square-headed windows were put in. In the sanctuary a fine sedilia was installed on the south side, with an Easter sepulchre on the north. A large slab of Frosterley marble was placed here in 1867, which reminds us of John Leyland's description of the beautiful Frosterley marble high altar slab, which he saw just before its destruction in 1548; the font base is also of Frosterley marble. Thomas Langley, who became Bishop of Durham in 1406, had the fine choir stalls put in. They have nine stalls on each side and display some excellent carved misericords.

In the 1860s, the church was thoroughly and sympathetically restored under George Gilbert Scott (1811–78). A nave altar, designed by Ronald Sims, was installed in 1975.

ST JOHN, ESCOMB

COUNTY DURHAM

ABOVE: *The early sundial on the south side of the church is unique.*

BELOW: *The church sits in a circular tree-lined churchyard.*

This uniquely well-preserved early Anglo-Saxon church has become justly renowned in the last century or so – until 1879 it was unknown and in a semi-ruined state. The porch now contains sculpture and fragments from gravestones; an excellent text written by Professor Rosemary Cramp gives an up-to-date interpretation of the history and archaeology of the building.

Although it was not mentioned by Bede, the church was probably erected in the 7th century within a roughly circular churchyard on the site of an earlier pagan or Roman shrine just to the south of the River Wear. It was almost entirely constructed with reused Roman masonry, which was taken from the nearby Roman fort at Binchester (Vinovia). Many of the stones have traces of Roman tool-marks on them and some reveal fragmentary inscriptions.

The church, with its very tall walls, simple nave and eastern sanctuary, is about 60 feet (20 metres) long. Originally, it also had a western chamber, which was demolished in about 1700, but the plan of this room was discovered during a recent excavation. The chamber's roofline is visible on the west wall of the church. The chancel arch is original and its voussoir blocks may have been taken directly from a Roman predecessor. Beneath it are the remains of medieval painted decoration on plaster. The rest of the plaster was removed in the 19th century, and, rather unnecessarily, the inside walls have recently been whitewashed.

The nave still contains its original square-headed north and south doorways, and two deeply splayed windows on both the north and south sides – those on the north are square-headed, while those on the south side are round. The walls of the nave were very slightly heightened and stepped gables were made in the 1490s, which was also when a new timber roof, dated recently using dendrochronology, was built. The windows in the nave and sanctuary date from the 13th century and 19th century, the latter being the large openings on the east, west and south. The south porch is a medieval addition and has a 17th-century sundial above its south wall doorway. Of unique importance is the Anglo-Saxon sundial, which can be seen in the middle of the nave's south wall; it is perhaps the earliest in-situ sun-dial in Britain. It breaks up the daylight hours into four quarters, and probably indicates that there was a small monastic community here from the beginning of the church's existence.

The building has been a parish church since the 12th century, but perhaps because of the close proximity of the Bishop of Durham's town and great residence at Auckland, it was never rebuilt or enlarged.

BELOW: *It is thought that the stones in the chancel arch may have been taken directly from a Roman arch.*

ST PAUL, JARROW

COUNTY DURHAM

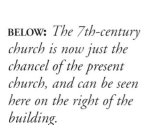

ABOVE: *An Anglo-Saxon doorway remains remarkably intact in the ruined cloister on the south side of the church.*

BELOW: *The 7th-century church is now just the chancel of the present church, and can be seen here on the right of the building.*

arrow lies in a post-industrial landscape, close to the south bank of the mouth of the River Tyne, 6 miles (10km) east of Newcastle. The famous ecclesiastical historian, the Venerable Bede, lived here for almost the whole of his life. A monastery was first founded in AD 674 at nearby Monkwearmouth by Benedict Biscop (*c.* AD 628–89), a Northumbrian nobleman who travelled to Rome several times and became abbot of Canterbury's famous monastery of St Peter and St Paul (later St Augustine's Abbey) under Archbishop Theodore. In AD 681, Biscop was given a second site at Jarrow, forming a double monastery. The dedicatory inscription can still be seen in the church. It describes 'the dedication of the basilica of St Paul on the 9th of the Kalends of May in the 15th year of King Egfrid' (i.e. 23 April AD 684 or 685). This inscription was originally set in the western part of the church, which was very sadly demolished in 1782, having survived for over 1,100 years. The nave of the present church, which was built by George Gilbert Scott in 1866, roughly covers the site of the old church. Some of the foundations of this first church were excavated in the 1970s, and it was found to have a series of chapels on either side.

Remarkably a second church was built to the east of the original one at about the same time,

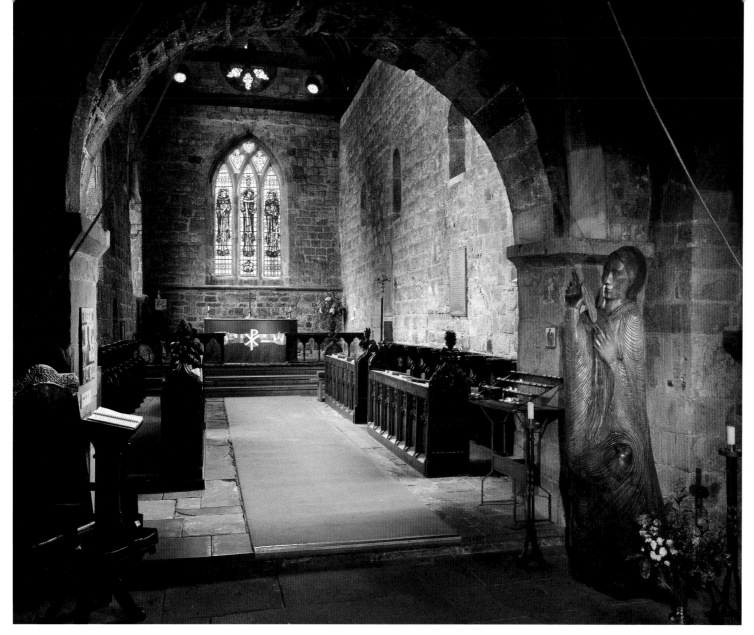

ABOVE: *The Norman arch leads through to the chancel, the shell of which dates from the 7th century.*

and much of this long narrow structure still survives as the chancel of the present church. Most notable is the south wall, which was built from reused Roman masonry – Hadrian's Wall and two Roman forts were nearby – and still contains three very small round-headed windows with frames for glass. Anglo-Saxon stained glass was discovered during excavations. It is probably the oldest such glass found in Britain and it was restored to one of the windows in 1980.

This second church was originally a completely separate building, but in the 11th century it was joined to the eastern end of the original basilica when a tower was installed. The monastery at Jarrow flourished in the late 7th and 8th centuries, with Bede studying and writing his many books here. However, in AD 794 the Vikings pillaged the monastery and many other attacks followed. The monastery was restored in 1074, but a decade later a large new monastery was established at Durham Cathedral, and the monks from Jarrow and Monkwearworth were transferred there. Bede's body, which originally lay here, was transferred to Durham Cathedral in the early 11th century. The two original monasteries became small cells of Durham's priory and after the Dissolution of the Monasteries became ordinary parish churches.

LEFT: *The famous dedicatory inscription of AD 684 or 685.*

OPPOSITE, RIGHT: *The concoction of old planks on the north side of the sanctuary is called, very inaccurately, 'Bede's chair'.*

227

ST ANDREW, CORBRIDGE

NORTHUMBERLAND

etween the late 1st century and the early 5th century AD, a sequence of Roman forts and towns, which acted as supply bases for Hadrian's Wall, existed close to Corbridge on a terrace above the River Tyne. By the 7th century these sites had been abandoned and stood in ruins, but an early Christian settlement was emerging on another promontory above the Tyne half a mile (0.8km) to the south-east. At the centre of this settlement, which may have been monastic from the beginning, was the present parish church. Remarkably the lower section of the western tower of the church and sections of the upper walls of the nave still survive from the original building. The tower was originally a western porch to the church, and the now blocked-up west doorway, with an original round-headed window above it, can still be seen in the west wall. The east wall of the tower still retains a fine original archway into the nave, which is almost entirely built of reused Roman masonry. The blocks of the arch itself are probably all taken from a dismantled Roman archway. Reused Roman masonry continued to be utilized for most of the later rebuildings of the church, up until at least the 14th century.

The original church included the western tower, a rectangular nave and small eastern sanctuary, and was similar to the church at Escomb in County Durham (see pages 224–5). Unlike Escomb's church, however, this one was rebuilt and enlarged many times between the 12th and 14th centuries. The south doorway, which is situated in the modern porch, dates from the early 12th century, and indicates that by this time the nave had already acquired a south aisle. By this point the church was a parish church and belonged to the newly founded Augustinian priory that was attached to Carlisle Cathedral. In the 13th century, a very long new chancel was built and this can best be seen from the south side, where there is a row of four lancet windows and a doorway between a line of large buttresses. In the later 13th century, up to the time of Edward I's wars in Scotland, the population of Corbridge expanded greatly. Transepts were built, followed by a whole series of aisles, including one on the north side of the chancel. Even the north transept was given a western aisle, as an afterthought. After this, the unstable nature of the English–Scottish border, which continued until the union of the two crowns in 1603, meant that little more was done to the church until major restoration took place in the 19th century. A rare survival, which points up the difficulties of the times, is the vicar's pele on the south side of the churchyard. This is a fortified tower residence that was provided for the vicar in the early 15th century. It still retains part of its crenellated parapets and machicolated corner turrets and was restored and re-roofed in 1910.

BELOW: *The church with its tall tower, which was originally a western porch, as seen from the south-east.*

ST MICHAEL, ALNWICK

NORTHUMBERLAND

ABOVE: *Fine Flemish wood carving can be found on this early 14th-century chest in the south aisle.*

BELOW: *The fine late 15th-century arcades in the chancel are enriched with elaborately carved capitals.*

T he town of Alnwick is dominated by the great castle of the dukes of Northumberland and a large triangular market-place. The parish church is on a rather peripheral site to the north-west. This is perhaps because the current market-place is a later addition; an earlier market was situated in Bailiffgate, the road between the church and the castle entrance. Just beyond this, Canongate leads north-west to the bridge over the Aln, and across the river is the site of Alnwick Abbey. This house of Premonstratensian canons, which was dissolved in 1539, provided the clergy for St Michael's church throughout the later Middle Ages.

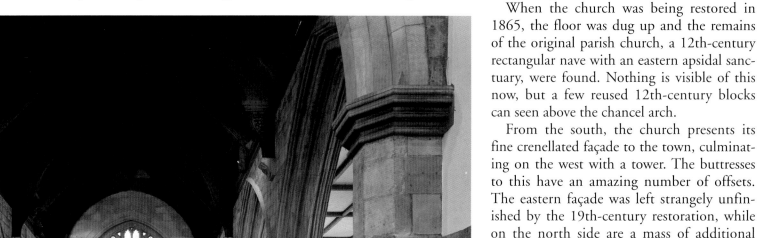

When the church was being restored in 1865, the floor was dug up and the remains of the original parish church, a 12th-century rectangular nave with an eastern apsidal sanctuary, were found. Nothing is visible of this now, but a few reused 12th-century blocks can seen above the chancel arch.

From the south, the church presents its fine crenellated façade to the town, culminating on the west with a tower. The buttresses to this have an amazing number of offsets. The eastern façade was left strangely unfinished by the 19th-century restoration, while on the north side are a mass of additional features, including, on the north-east, the Duke of Northumberland's private entrance porch, which is now a heating chamber!

Inside the building is a very large open space, with continuous aisles on either side. This is the church that was restored in 1863 by Anthony Salvin (1799–1881). He stripped out the post-medieval galleries, pews and other fittings, and tried to restore the church to its late 15th-century state. Despite the large amount of new masonry, including the chancel arch and east window, it is possible to see that the rebuilding and enlargement of the church started in the early 14th century on the north side of the nave, at about the time that Henry de Percy, the first of the Percys, bought the castle and barony of Alnwick from the Bishop of Durham in 1309. Work continued during the later 14th century with the building of the tower and enlarged south aisle. This was during the time of the very powerful Henry Percy (1342–1408), who became the 1st Earl of Northumberland in 1377. It was the 4th Earl, yet another Henry Percy (1446–89), who completely remodelled the chancel with its two very large flanking chapels. The magnificent late 15th-century arcades on either side of the chancel are the most impressive architectural details in the church. The four richly carved foliate capitals are particularly fine, and on the north-east the crescent and fetterlock of the Percys can be seen. Above the north side of this capital is the carved figure of St Catherine, with her wheel visible on her shield.

The church also contains a great deal of later 19th-century stained glass, but the most recent addition is the new font, which is made of Kilkenny limestone, and was dedicated in 2001.

BELOW: *The long, low church on the edge of Alnwick is the burial place of the earls and dukes of Northumberland.*

HOLY TRINITY, BERWICK-UPON-TWEED

NORTHUMBERLAND

ABOVE: *The Flemish glass of the west window was given to the church by Dudley Coutts Marjoribanks MP in the mid-19th century.*

BELOW: *The south front of the church boasts many Venetian windows. The polygonal turret on the left was added in the 19th century.*

erwick-upon-Tweed is a unique town at the extreme northern tip of England. It was fought over by the Scots and English for many centuries, and by 1603, when the two crowns were finally united with the accession of James I, it was surrounded by immensely strong ramparts. Between 1603 and 1634 the great bridge across the River Tweed was rebuilt, with some funds donated by the crown, and it was the king's wish that any surplus money should be spent on rebuilding the very small and dilapidated medieval church within the town. In 1641, Charles I agreed that the work should go ahead; however, the following year the Civil War started. Extra money for the work was collected, and the old Berwick Castle (where the railway station is now) was acquired, primarily for its building materials, although the initial intent was to build the new church here.

Holy Trinity church is tucked away in the north corner of Berwick, behind the very large 1858 Presbyterian Church of Scotland church on Wallace Green. In 1650, a year after the execution of the king, the town's Guild of Freeman contracted a London mason, John Young of Blackfriars, to build the new church, and over the course of the next two years the present church was constructed. The work was greatly helped by the Governor of Berwick, Colonel George Fenwick. The church was opened at the end of 1652, although the building of the church galleries continued for another five years.

This remarkable church, partly based on the church of St Katherine Cree in London, was built as a rectangular structure with north and south aisles inside and the pulpit to the south. It was simply a Puritan preaching box, without an altar, chancel, stained glass, organ, tower or bells. It included a mixture of very late Gothic elements – such as tracery windows at the east and west ends, which were later replaced – and some semi-

classical elements. When the church was eventually consecrated by the Bishop of Durham, John Cosin, two years after the Restoration of Charles II in 1660, he stipulated that the gallery on the east should be dismantled to accommodate a communion table and chancel. His demand was not carried out until 1855 when the present chancel was built and when many of the original Gothic windows were redesigned in a classical style. Nevertheless, the church font dates from 1662.

The tower was never built, and the bells are now rung in the 150-foot (45-metre) high mid-18th-century belfry on the town hall. The organ was installed in 1772, when the galleries and seating were reorganized. The big change, however, was the large-scale restoration of 1855. Not only were the chancel and vestry built, but some magnificent 16th- and 17th-century glass was inserted in a new west window and a 'proper' chancel and chancel arch were built. The galleries were not finally removed until 1905, when a new organ chamber was built on the north-east.

BELOW: *The arcades in the Commonwealth nave are of the Tuscan order.*

ST CUTHBERT, BEWCASTLE
CUMBRIA

ABOVE: *An 18th-century tombstone in the churchyard.*

BELOW AND BELOW, RIGHT: *The lower part of the west face of the cross-shaft depicts St John the Evangelist, while the south face has beautiful vinescroll carving.*

This remote little parish church, in the extreme north-west corner of England, has within its churchyard the finest Anglo-Saxon cross-shaft in the country. Only at Ruthwell, across the border in Scotland, does a comparable relic survive.

The site of Bewcastle, which lies above the Cam Beck, has a long history. In AD 122 a large Roman fort was built here as a forward defence to Hadrian's Wall – a Roman road from Bewcastle runs 6 miles (10km) to Birdoswald fort on the wall. The fort at Bewcastle was abandoned before the end of the 4th century, but by the 8th century monks probably sheltered here, although the

234

RIGHT: *The famous Bewcastle cross-shaft is surrounded by picturesque 18th- and 19th-century graves.*

BELOW RIGHT: *The late 18th-century west end of the church.*

only evidence of this is the cross. In 1092 William Rufus took Cumbria from the Scots and a small castle was built at the site, forming an outpost to the principal castle at Carlisle. The site of this castle was north of the church, in the north-east corner of the Roman fort, but all that can be seen today are the ruined walls of a later castle.

A parish church may first have been built here in the early 12th century, once the castle was completed. However, all that survives of the medieval church is the 13th-century chancel, with its restored lancet windows, which was partly built of reused stone from the Roman fort. The castle was in 'great ruin and decay' by the early 17th century, and the church also appears to have fallen into a sorry state. It was rebuilt in its present form in 1792 with a shortened nave and a new west tower at the north end of the west wall.

As this region was frequently overrun by the English and Scots armies and border-raiders between the 12th and 17th centuries, it is a miracle that the magnificent Anglo-Saxon cross has survived at all. The cross-head had disappeared by the early 17th century, but the shaft survives in good condition – it is 14 feet (4 metres) high on its square base. On each face are different panels of decoration, including beautiful vine scrolls, interlacing and chequer patterns containing grapes, birds and beasts. The quality of the carving is extremely high, with the south face featuring a sundial. The principal face is the west one, and displays St John the Evangelist in a shallow arched recess at the bottom. Above this is a long and almost illegible runic inscription that refers to King Alcfrith, son of Oswi (who is known to have died in AD 670). Higher still, is a carving of the figure of Christ, standing on two beasts and holding a scroll and at the top is a carving of St John the Baptist with the Lamb of God. These two recessed panels are separated by the words 'Jesus Christ' in runic script.

GLOSSARY

AMBULATORY Processional walk round the eastern arm of a large church, especially the aisle enclosing an apse

APSE Semicircular recess, usually on the east, for an altar

ARCADE Series of arches

BAY Section of wall between external buttresses and internal piers

BOSS Large, usually carved, knob at the intersection of vault ribs

CAPITAL The top, often decorated, section of a column

CHANCEL The eastern part of the church, beyond the screen containing the choir and sanctuary

CHANTRY CHAPEL Special chapel created for an important person or family in which a priest said masses for the deceased. Abolished by law during the Reformation of 1548

CHEVRON V-shaped carved decoration, common on 12th-century arches or piers

CHOIR Area of stalls at the west end of the chancel from which services are said or sung

CLERESTORY Windowed upper part of a wall, above the aisle roofs

CORBEL Large projecting block, usually of stone and often carved

CROSSING Area, often under a tower, between the north and south transepts. Sometimes the choir is here

CRYPT Hidden space below a sanctuary, usually in the eastern arm or below an aisle

DECORATED English architectural style from c. 1290 to c. 1350, taking its name from the type of tracery used at this time

EARLY ENGLISH English architectural style from c. 1175 to c. 1245, when the pointed arch (and the Gothic style) made its first appearance

EASTER SEPULCHRE Tomb-like recess on the north side of the sanctuary, holding the Reserved Sacrament between Maundy Thursday and Easter Sunday

FAN-VAULT Vault of concave semicones without ribs

GEOMETRIC English architectural style from c. 1245 to c. 1290, taking its name from the form of tracery used at this time

GOTHIC Name given to medieval architecture between c. 1175 and c. 1540 – sub-phases are Early English, Geometric, Decorated and Perpendicular

LADY CHAPEL Chapel in honour of the Blessed Virgin Mary and, from the 13th century, usually the most important chapel in a church

LANCET Tall late 12th- to 13th-century window with a pointed head

LIERNE VAULT Vault with small extra ribs in the upper part

LUCARNE A window appearing in the spire

MISERICORD Carved bracket on the lower side of a hinged stall seat to support a standing occupant of the stall

NAVE The body or western part of a church, usually with aisles.

PARAPET Low wall on top of a large wall at the base of a roof

PARCLOSE A screen enclosing an altar or tomb or to separate a chapel from the rest of the church

PERPENDICULAR English architectural style from c. 1340 to c. 1540

PIER Supporting pillar in an arcade

PISCINA Shallow basin with a drain for washing vessels used during Mass, usually in a wall to the south of an altar

RECTOR Formerly a patron or independent incumbent who received tithes and was responsible for the chancel and rectory.

REREDOS Screen or wall-decoration behind and above an altar

RIB-VAULT Projecting feature of a vault

ROMANESQUE Architectural style in western Europe of the 11th and 12th centuries, when the round arch was used; often called 'Norman' in England

ROOD The crucifixion, flanked by St Mary and St John, usually on top of a beam or Rood screen at the eastern end of the nave. Destroyed by law in 1548, but are sometimes found in 19th- and 20th-century churches

SANCTUARY Small eastern end of an early church with the high altar at the centre. To the north was often the Easter Sepulchre, and to the south the sedilia

SEDILIA Usually three canopied seats, for priests, on the south side of the sanctuary

TESTER Flat wooden board or canopy over a pulpit, tomb or shrine

TIERCERON VAULT Vault with three extra ribs springing from the corners of the bays

TRACERY Intersecting ribs on vaults, blank arches, or in the upper part of a window

TRANSEPTS North and south projections, usually from the crossing, in a church. They sometimes have aisles

TRIFORIUM Gallery, usually above the aisles and with a lean-to roof

VAULT Arched ceiling, usually with ribs of stone or timber

VICAR Rector's deputy, who became the parish priest once the church had become appropriated by its patron

VOUSSOIR A wedge-like stone that forms part of an arch

CONTACT DETAILS

THE SOUTH-WEST

ST MATERIANA
Tintagel, Cornwall
PL34 0DL

ST ANIETUS
St Neot, Cornwall
PL14 6NA

ST NONNA
Altarnun, Cornwall
PL15 7SJ
Tel: 01566 86108

ST MARY MAGDALENE
Tower Street, Launceston,
Cornwall PL15 8AU
Tel: 01566 774533

ST ANDREW
Community House,
1a Church Street,
Cullompton, Devon
EX15 1JU
Tel: 01884 33249

Fax: 01884 34747
churchoffice@
cullompton.org
www.cullompton.org/
standrews

ST MARY
Ottery St Mary, Devon
EX11 1DQ
Tel: 01404 812999
churchoffice@o-s-m.net
www.otterystmary.org.uk

ST WINIFRED
Branscombe, Devon EX12
Tel: 01297 680364

ST GEORGE
The Rectory, St George's
Street, Dunster, Somerset
TA24 6RS

ST MARY
Stogumber, Somerset TA4
Tel: 01984 656262

www.stogumber.org.uk/
church.htm

ST MARY
Isle Abbots, Somerset TA3
Tel: 01460 57811
info@it-anglican.org
www.it-anglican.org

ST BARTHOLOMEW
Crewkerne, Somerset
vicar@stbartholomew-
crewkerne.org
www.stbartholomew-
crewkerne.org

ST NICHOLAS
Studland, Dorset BH19

ST NICHOLAS
Moreton, Dorset DT2

ST JOHN THE BAPTIST
Bere Regis, Wareham,
Dorset BH20 7HQ

Tel: 01929 471262
www.bereregiswithaffpud-
dle.org.uk

ST CUTHBURGA
Wimborne Minster, High
Street, Wimborne, Dorset
BH21 1HT
Tel: 01202 884753
www.wimborneminster.
org.uk

ST MARY
Breamore, Hampshire SP6

ALL SAINTS
East Meon,
Hampshire GU32

ST MARY
Brading,
Isle of Wight PO36

ST THOMAS THE MARTYR
Parish Office, St Thomas's
House, St Thomas's Square,
Salisbury SP1 1BA
Tel: 01722 322537
www.stthomassalisbury.
co.uk

ST MARY, ST KATHARINE
AND ALL SAINTS
Edington, Wiltshire BA13

ST MARY
Potterne, Wiltshire SN10
church@potterne.net

ST MARY REDCLIFFE
12 Colston Parade, Bristol,
Avon BS1 6RA
Tel: 0117 9291487
parish.office@
stmaryredcliffe.co.uk
www.stmaryredcliffe.co.uk

**THE WESTERN
COUNTIES**

ST MARY
Church Road, Ewelme,
Oxfordshire OX10 6HS

ST MARY
The Rectory, Church Way,
Iffley, Oxfordshire
OX4 4EJ
Tel: 01865 773516

ST MARY
High Street, Oxford,
Oxfordshire OX1 4AH
Tel: 01865 279111
university.church@ox.ac.uk
www.university-
church.ox.ac.uk

ST MARY
Uffington,
Oxfordshire SN7

ST JOHN THE BAPTIST
Church Green, Burford,
Oxfordshire OX18 4RY
Tel: 01993 823788

ST MARY
Fairford,
Gloucestershire GL7
Tel: 01285 712611
st.marysfairford@
btconnect.com

ST JOHN THE BAPTIST
Parish Office, 1 Coxwell
Street, Cirencester,
Gloucestershire GL7 2BQ
Tel: 01285 659317
Fax: 01285 641621
parishoffice@acinc.org.uk
www.acinc.org.uk/
parish-ch.htm

ST MARY
Deerhurst, Gloucestershire
GL19 4DQ
Tel: 01452 780880

ST MARY
Kempley,
Gloucestershire GL18
Tel: 01531 660214
customers@english-
heritage.org.uk
www.english-
heritage.org.uk

ST MICHAEL
Church Lane, Ledbury,
Herefordshire HR8
Tel: 01531 631531
ledbury.ministry@
virgin.net

ST MARY AND ST DAVID
Kilpeck, Herefordshire
HR2 9DW
www.herefordwebpages.co.
uk/kilpeck.shtml

ST PETER AND ST PAUL
The Team Office, The
Verger's House, Church
Street, Leominster,
Herefordshire HR6 8NH
Tel: 01568 612124

ST LAURENCE
College Street, Ludlow,
Shropshire SY8 1AN
Tel: 01584 872073
rector@stlaurences.org.uk
www.stlaurences.org.uk

ST MARY
Acton Burnell,
Shropshire SY5
Tel: 01743 872251

ST MARY
St Mary's Street,
Shrewsbury, Shropshire
SY1 1EG
Tel: 01743 357006

ST MARY
Old Square, Warwick,
Warwickshire CV34 4RA
Tel: 01926 400771
www.stmaryswarwick.
org.uk

THE SOUTH-EAST

HOLY TRINITY
Bosham, Sussex
PO18 8HX
Tel: 01243 573228
Fax: 01243 573228

ST MARY DE HAURA
New Shoreham, Sussex
BN43 5DQ
Tel: 01273 452109
www.stmarydehaura.org.uk
info@stmarydehaura.org.uk

ST SAVIOUR AND ST PETER
South Street, Eastbourne,
Sussex BN21 4UT
Tel: 01323 729702
www.st-saviours.org

ST PETER
Ashburnham, Battle,
Sussex TN33 9NF
Tel: 01424 773073

ST THOMAS
St Thomas Street,
Winchelsea, East Sussex
TN36 4EB
Tel: 01797 226254

ST NICHOLAS
Church Road, New
Romney, Kent TN28 8EY
Tel: 01797 362308

ST MARY
Brook, Kent TN25
Tel: 01233 812450

ST MARTIN
Church Street, St Pauls,
Canterbury, Kent
CT1 1NH
Tel: 01227 462686

ST MARY
Stone, Kent TN25
Tel: 01322 382 076

ST MARY
Stoke D'Abernon, Surrey
KT11 3PU
Tel: 01932 869922
theverger@stmarys
cottage.freeserve.co.uk

ST NICHOLAS
The Street, Compton,
Surrey GU3 1ED
Tel: 01483 810328

ST MARY
Church Hill,
Harrow-on-the-Hill,
Harrow, London

HA1 3HL
Tel: 020 8422 2652

ST MARY
High Street,
Harmondsworth,
Middlesex UB7 OA4

ST JOHN
Shottesbrooke, Berkshire
SL6 3SW

ALL SAINTS
Church Street, Wing,
Buckinghamshire
LU7 0NX

ST MICHAEL
Stewkley,
Buckinghamshire LU7

ALL SAINTS
Hillesden,
Buckinghamshire MK18
Tel: 01280 813162

ST MARY
Felmersham,
Bedfordshire MK43
Tel: 01234 309737
david@devon.powernet.
co.uk (Revd David Mason)

ST ETHELDREDA
Hatfield,
Hertfordshire AL10
Tel: 01707 267531

**THE EASTERN
COUNTIES**

ST PETER
Bradwell-on-Sea, Essex
CM10 7PX
Tel: 01621 776203
www.bradwellchapel.org

ST MICHAEL
Church Road, Copford,
Essex CO6 1DA
Tel: 01206 210488

HOLY TRINITY
Church Walk,
Long Melford, Suffolk
CO10 9DL
Tel: 01787 310845

ST PETER AND ST PAUL
Lavenham, Suffolk CO10

ST MICHAEL
Church Street,
Framlingham, Suffolk
IP13

HOLY TRINITY
Blythburgh, Suffolk IP19

ST EDMUND, KING AND
MARTYR
The Common, Southwold,
Suffolk IP18 6AH
Tel: 01787 247206

ST MARGARET
Cley next the Sea,
Norfolk NR25

ST MARGARET
The Saturday Market
Place, King's Lynn,
Norfolk PE30 5EB
Tel: 01553 772858

ST MARY
West Walton, Norfolk
PE14
WestWalton@voci.co.uk
www.ely.anglican.org/
parishes/westwalton

ST PETER AND ST PAUL
Church Terrace, Wisbech,
Cambridgeshire PE13 1BJ
Tel: 01945 582508

ST MARY
Church Street, Ickleton,
Saffron Walden, Essex
CB10 1SL
Tel: 01799 506024
Rector.saffronwalden@
ntlworld.com
www.stmaryssaffron-
walden.org

**THE CENTRAL
COUNTIES**

ST PETER
Northampton,
Northamptonshire NN1

ALL SAINTS
Station Road, Brixworth,
Northampton NN6 9DF
Tel: 01604 880286

ST MARY
Wood Street, Higham
Ferrers, Rushden,
Northamptonshire
NN10 8DL
Tel: 01933 312433

ST MARY AND ST
HARDULPH
The Rectory, Rectory
Close, Breedon-on-the-
Hill, Derby, Derbyshire
DE73 1BY
Tel: 01332 865476

ST MARY
Main Street, Chadwell,
Melton Mowbray,
Leicestershire LE14 4QN

ST WULFRAM
The Vestry, Church Street,
Grantham, Lincolnshire
NG31 6RR
Tel: 01476 561342

ST BOTOLPH
Market Place, Boston,
Lincolnshire
Tel: 01205 362992

ST HELEN
Brant Broughton,
Lincolnshire LN5
Tel: 01400 273987

ST JAMES
The Parish Office,
6 Upgate, Louth,
Lincolnshire LN11 6ET
Tel: 01507 610247
Fax: 01507 602991
www.stjameschurchlouth.
com

ST MARY
St Mary's Rectory,
Normanby Road, Stow,
Lincolnshire LN1 2DF
Tel: 01427 788251
www.stowminster.org.uk

ST MARY MAGDALENE
The Vestry, Market Place,
Newark-on-Trent,
Nottinghamshire
NG24 1DU
Tel: 01636 704513

**THE NORTHERN
COUNTIES**

ST EDITHA
Church Street, Tamworth,
Staffordshire B79 7BX
Tel: 01827 62446

ST MICHAEL AND ST MARY
Church Square,
Melbourne, Derby,
Derbyshire DE73 1EN
Tel: 01332 862347

ST WYSTAN
Repton, Derbyshire DE65

ST OSWALD
Ashbourne,
Derbyshire DE6
Tel: 01335 343129
www.ashbourneparish.org

ST MARY AND ALL SAINTS
Church Way, Chesterfield,
Derbyshire S40 1XJ
Tel: 01246 206506
www.chesterfield-
parishchurch.org.uk

ST MICHAEL
Market Place, Macclesfield
SK10 1HW
Tel: 01625 421984
maccteamparish@
surefish.co.uk
www.stmichaels-
macclesfield.com

ST MARY
Church Lane, Nantwich,
Cheshire CW5 5RQ
Tel: 01270 625268
StMarysNantwich@
btinternet.com

www.stmarysnantwich.
btinternet.co.uk

ST JOHN THE BAPTIST
Chester, Cheshire CH1

ST MARY
Church Lane, Whalley,
Lancashire BB7 9SY
Tel: 01254 823249
office@whalleypc.com
www.whalleypc.com

ST PATRICK
Patrington, Yorkshire (East
Riding) HU12
Tel: 01964 60313

ST MARY
Lastingham, North
Yorkshire YO6
Tel: 01751 417344
vicarage@
lastinghamchurch.org.uk
www.lastinghamchurch.
org.uk

ST MARY
Whitby,
North Yorkshire YO21

ST CUTHBERT
St Cuthbert's Centre,
Market Place, Darlington,
County Durham
DL1 5QG
Tel: 01325 482417

ST JOHN
Escomb,
County Durham DL14

ST PAUL
Church Bank, Jarrow,
County Durham
Tel: 0191 4897052

ST ANDREW
Market Place, Corbridge,
Northumberland
NE45 5DW
Tel: 01434 632979

ST MICHAEL
Bailiffgate, Alnwick,
Northumberland
NE66 1LZ
Tel: 01665 602797

HOLY TRINITY
The Vicarage, Parade,
Berwick-upon-Tweed,
Northumberland
TD15 1DF
berwick.church@
bigwig.net

ST CUTHBERT
Bewcastle, Cumbria CA6
Tel: 01699 748660

237

INDEX

238